GIRALDI CINTHIO
ON ROMANCES

GIRALDI CINTHIO
ON ROMANCES

Being a translation of the
Discorso intorno al comporre dei romanzi
with introduction & notes by
HENRY L. SNUGGS

UNIVERSITY OF KENTUCKY PRESS
LEXINGTON 1968

Copyright © 1968 by the University of Kentucky Press
Library of Congress Catalog Card No. 68-12971

To
Allan H. Gilbert
Tutti lo miran, tutti onor gli fanno

PREFACE

Giovambattista Giraldi's *Discorso intorno al comporre dei romanzi* (dated by the author as completed in 1549; published in Venice in 1554, along with Giraldi's earlier *Discorso . . . delle comedie et delle tragedie*), having exerted a great impact, direct and indirect, on subsequent poetry as well as theory, is an important document in the history of criticism. The work, however, is not generally available to those interested in the theory of literature, at least to those who find sixteenth-century Italian a formidable linguistic barrier. The only English translation of the work consists of approximately ten selected pages of the 198 of the 1554 text translated by Allan H. Gilbert in his *Literary Criticism: Plato to Dryden*, except for short quotations in such works as Bernard Weinberg's *A History of Literary Criticism of the Italian Renaissance*.

There are problems, moreover, even for those who are able to overcome the linguistic barrier, for copies of the 1554 edition are extremely rare, and most of them are lodged in the rare-book collections of large libraries. Only one other edition is known. In 1864 G. Daelli published *Scritti Estetici di Giambattista Giraldi Cintio* in two parts, the first being the *Discorso . . . dei romanzi*. Regrettably copies of this edition have also become very scarce.

In view of this situation I have here presented an English translation of Giraldi's *Discorso . . . dei romanzi*, with an introduction that attempts to interpret the theory of literature Giraldi gave us and with notes that aim at identifying or explaining Giraldi's numerous references and allusions to literature and people of the western world, ancient, medieval, and Renaissance.

The translation is based on both the 1554 and the 1864 editions. The latter includes interpolations by Giraldi in a printed copy of the 1554 edition still extant in the Biblioteca Comunale Ariostea at Ferrara. Giulio Antimaco, the editor of the 1864 edition, in his "Avvertenza dell' Editore," describes his experience in transcribing, with the assistance of the librarian, Giraldi's marginal notes and MS pages of additions. Many of the marginal notes, the librarian Signor Cittadella wrote to Antimaco, have been "mutilated from handling by a most careless binder" so that it was necessary to guess at the mutilated or missing words. Antimaco decided, he says, not to try conjectures about these lacunae but to include the interpolated passages in his text as they were, "leaving its restoration to more fortunate and courageous conjecturers, if it will be worth the effort."

My own study of Giraldi's additions included in Antimaco's 1864 text has led me to these conclusions about them. The short ones, usually of a single word or phrase, are additions rather than substitutions; generally they aid either in clarifying his meaning or in amplifying his statements. The longer ones are not on the whole well integrated with the original 1554 text. Exploring some related matter, they say little not already stated in the original text. Some of these longer ones, as Cittadella and Antimaco said, have so many lacunae as to be unintelligible. The additions give the impression of hasty writing; their style is laxer and less formal than the original and often clashes with it. They add little to the critical statements. It is possible that these interpolations and additions were not intended for printing but for lectures.

In the light of my conclusions, I have incorporated the short additions in the translation. The longer ones, which are at times digressive, are given in the appendix.

I completed the research for and the writing of this work while a Fellow of the Southeastern Institute of Medieval and Renaissance Studies at the University of North Carolina (at Chapel Hill) and Duke University in the summers of 1965 and 1966. I wish to thank Professor John L. Lievsay of Duke University, co-chairman of the Institute, for many helpful suggestions and also the staffs of the two university libraries for their aid and courtesy. I am also grateful to Wake Forest University for a grant in aid of research and publication.

November 1966 H. L. S.

CONTENTS

Preface *vii*

Introduction *xiii*

Giraldi Cinthio on Romances 1

Appendix 165

Notes 179

Index 191

INTRODUCTION

In the dedicatory letter to Ruggieri, Giraldi wrote that his chief aim in the *Discourse* was to refute the attacks on Ariosto's *Orlando Furioso*. Giraldi was convinced that the *Furioso* not only was a great poem but was a great heroic poem. To defend Ariosto, therefore, his discourse presents both an inquiry into the very nature of poetry and into the characteristics of the genre in which some of the world's richest poems fall. His title is a little misleading, for although he was really writing a theory of the heroic poem, he had to use the term *romance* to communicate his meaning because of its currency in his own time, knowing the difficulties which its connotations would create for him.

In the hands of a great artist, the poet Ariosto, a heroic poem equal to those of the ancients had evolved out of the raw, often crude materials called *romanzi*. This vast formless matter was so vulgar or popular that, as Giraldi said, even the makers of carpet slippers tried their hands at it. Giraldi did not have the benefit of the modern theory of how the Homeric poems came into being out of the vast saga material which lies back of the *Iliad* and the *Odyssey*, but he anticipates this theory in some respects in his theory of the development of the heroic poem in his time out of the medieval and early Renaissance *romanzi* matter.

But the *Iliad* and the *Odyssey*, though undeniably great poems, are lacking, says Giraldi, in the decorum that must inform poems of ultimate artistry. Giraldi's critical view of Homer is remarkably like Dryden's view of Shakespeare —a great poet but lacking in art. The ancient heroic poem reached perfection in the *Aeneid*, which embodies the decorum lacking in the Homeric poems. In his exaltation of Vergil as the greatest of poets, Giraldi is thoroughly a part of his age.

For Giraldi there are critical principles that constitute poetics or the art of poetry, and these primary laws were "discovered not devised" by such critics as Aristotle and Horace, and developed and amplified in his age by critics such as Bembo. But there is a distinction between primary laws true in any age, for all time, the "needful rules" (as Ben Jonson later put it), and those applicable only to one age. The law of unity, for example, is primary, and Aristotle stated this principle; but the kind of unity that Aristotle observed in the *Iliad* and the *Odyssey*, though true of these poems and in that respect good, is really a particular kind in particular poems, not the primary law of unity. The single-action heroic poem is unified, but there can be another kind of unity in the heroic poem of multiple actions. So, while there are primary or universal laws of poetry, each age develops its own particular laws, good for that age but subject to modification in another.

Implicit in this distinction between universal and particular critical principles is the theory of genres. Every poem is in essence like some others written before it; every poem also has its unique, individual quality. For Giraldi one of the basic genres is the "epic" or "heroic," first defined by Aristotle. But since the *Orlando Furioso* grew out of what were called *romanzi*, Giraldi retains that term both in title and text, using it synonymously with "heroic poem" to describe the genre as it had developed in his time. As seems clear from the *Discourse*, the *Iliad*, the

Odyssey, the *Aeneid*, and the *Orlando Furioso* are all heroic poems; and if Giraldi could have known the *Gerusalemme Liberata*, *The Faerie Queene*, and *Paradise Lost*, he would have included these poems in the same genre.

⁂

Giraldi framed his *Discourse* in the traditional theory of oratory with its three aspects, invention, disposition, and elocution, but the *Discourse* breaks out of this frame, and there is on the whole little reference to oratory. Giraldi thus contributes to the gradual emancipation during the sixteenth century of poetic theory from the oratorical tradition.

For Giraldi the essence of poetry inheres in its fictionality. It is neither history nor philosophy, even though the heroic poem may be based on history and even though philosophical ideas may be embodied in it. Invention by the poet is primary; the fable is to the poem as the skeleton is to the body. Poetry, for Giraldi, is nonassertive statement. Though verisimilitude is a characteristic of it, poetry is the feigning of what ought to be or could be, not the relating of what is; its essence lies in the creation of fiction. Like many others Giraldi finds the fictional, the poetic, to be more verisimilar than the factual, i.e., more like the truth.

⁂

Giraldi's theory of poetry is organic. The poem is likened to the human being, body and soul. Just as the skeleton alone does not make up a human being, so the idea or subject or fable (the original invention) alone does not make the poem. The poem must be structured as the skeleton is held together by the ligaments. This second principle, that of disposition in the oratorical tradition, produces the structural order, which is inseparable from the idea or subject. Giraldi sustains the figure in likening the "substance" of a poem to the flesh and its "ornaments" to the skin. Ornamentation is the third principle, to which he assigns the familiar oratorical term *elocution* and to which he devotes at least half of the *Discourse*. Though he employs the terms *ornament* and *elocution*, these are not really at odds with his organic theory. Language and what language conveys are inseparable. A poem is a verbal construct which conveys its artistic effect not merely by its semantic quality but also by its euphony and rhythm. The "words" are not just neutral signs, as in purely discursive statement, but have their inherent qualities as symbols. These are "ornamental" in the way the skin is, but at the same time are as organic to the poem as the skin to the life of the body.

The nature of poetic statement, then, is fictionality conveyed as a total ordered structure in figurative, euphonious, and metrically rhythmical language. The poem approaches art to the degree that it is an organic whole in which all the constituent "parts" are interdependent and really inseparable. The poet considers not only the whole but "how each particular part may be placed with beautiful order and grace and proportion" in relation to the whole.

Closely related to—almost a part of—the principle of organic unity is the principle of decorum, which is, as Giraldi says, "not otherwise than grace and appropriateness" in the whole and in every particular as part of the whole. This principle is applicable to all artistic expression. Though nature is always primary, it must be aided by and united with art. In large part art consists in the knowledge of what is appropriate and the ability to effect this knowledge in composition. Much of the *Discourse* is on this subject, especially on the special aspects of decorum applicable to the heroic poem. The poet must exercise decorum not only in general but in each genre of poetry, since the creation of a poem of a certain genre demands a sense of what is fitting for the genre.

ஓ

Giraldi follows the Aristotelian principle that poetry has its origin in imitation or mimesis. Poetry is all imitation, he says, and imitation and verse serve to distinguish poetic statement from that which is not. The general theory of imitation occupies little of the *Discourse*, however, since he is interested not so much in the original theory in the *Poetics* as in the Horatian-Renaissance doctrine (always named imitation) that the poet should emulate the great poems with a view to equaling or even surpassing them in art.

This particular doctrine of imitation pervades the *Discourse*. Though poetry has its origin in the *furor poeticus*, or enthusiasm, even this may be and often is induced by reading a great poem. Though good poetry cannot be written without this infused spirit, it must be accompanied by art. One acquires the good judgment that is the source of art in two ways: first, by conversing with good writers and learning from them, as a pupil from a master; second, by observing the writing of those authors regarded as excellent, discerning their virtues, and seeking with all studiousness to emulate them. The greatest of all emulators or imitators was Vergil, who acquired all the virtues and avoided all the faults of Homer and of others and thus surpassed his master. (Not only Giraldi but many other sixteenth-century critics held the view that Vergil was greater than Homer.)

❧

The *Discourse* insists that poetry is an art. Dominant in Giraldi's statement of the function of the art of poetry is the pleasure the reader or hearer derives from the beautiful artistic effect of a poem. Throughout the work he stays close to the esthetic value of poetry. He usually includes "hearer" as well as "reader" since he is ever conscious of the living language, of both its euphony and its metrical rhythm. Much of the *Discourse* minutely analyzes euphonious and rhythmical effects in poems, especially those of Petrarch, Bembo, and Ariosto. Recurring throughout are such phrases as "wonderful delight" and "pleasurable artistic effect." *Vaghezza*, in the sense of beauty, charm, grace, is always prominent in his statements about these poems. The total impact is that pleasure is the chief aim of poetry, that the esthetic is its dominant function.

Nevertheless Giraldi is very much a part of his age, or, perhaps one should say, a shaper of his age, for equally prominent in his statement of the function of poetry are the Horatian concepts known as *utile* and *dulci*. Phrases such as "profit and delight," "the useful and the delightful" recur throughout. Poetry for him has a civil function, to instruct in good customs or manners (in the older meaning of the term), to shape the mores of civilization. The end of composing for any poet, he says, is "to teach men honest life and good customs." He anticipates Sidney and, of course, many other critics in saying that whereas ethical philosophy teaches an honest and praiseworthy life in a rational assertion, poetry does it better and more delightfully under the veil of a fable. Poetry therefore confers all the benefits of philosophy and, as art, is superior to it. As one can see, Giraldi is as well grounded in the *Poetics* as in the *Ars Poetica*.

ぇ◆

The *Discourse* is really about the heroic poem in Giraldi's own time—concretely the *Orlando Furioso*—and also about the ideal heroic poem visualized for the future. Several observations about Giraldi's theory will serve to emphasize its significant contribution to the theory of literature and its impact, direct or indirect, on subsequent heroic poems.

First, he says, a great heroic poem equal to those of Homer and Vergil exists in modern times; other great heroic poems, he implies, will be written in the future. Giraldi makes the first significant plea in sixteenth-century criticism for the poetry of that (and our) time. Most critical statements prior to and contemporary with the *Discourse*, when discussing the heroic poem, spoke solely of the ancient. Giraldi talks about Boiardo, Ariosto, even Trissino (though his opinion of the last is rather low). Of poetry of other genres, he writes about the verse of Petrarch, Bembo, Della Casa, Politian, Benivieni, and many others. These are poets like Horace, Ovid, Propertius, and Tibullus. The sonnet and the canzone are as respectable and authentic poetic art as the ode and the epithalamium. In critical theory Bembo's *Prose* rivals Aristotle's *Rhetoric* and Quintilian's *Institutes*. Giraldi led the way to the recognition of the modern; others followed him—Minturno in *L'Arte Poetica* (1563/4), Mazzoni in the *Difesa* (1572)—but Giraldi's *Discourse* remains as the earlier and more cogent assertion of the literature of his own age.

The modern heroic poem cannot imitate the ancient in every respect; it must adapt itself to modern times. The principles of both decorum and verisimilitude require the modern heroic poem to reflect the mores of its own age. The supernatural machinery of the Homeric poems, for example, with its gods and goddesses behaving like sensual human beings, though truly poetic in the context of the Homeric age, cannot be carried over into the modern heroic, which should be based on the Christian religion. To have God behave like Zeus and archangels like Poseidon or Aphrodite would not only violate decorum but border on impiety. Nor could Angelica, a princess, wash clothes like Nausicaa, the daughter of King Alcinous. If the poet wishes to use Homeric or other ancient materials, he should imitate Vergil, whose Trojans are essentially like Romans of the Augustan age in customs and general mode of life.

But the necessity of adapting the heroic poem to what is appropriate to its own time does not mean the creation of a new genre. The *romanzo* as developed in such a poem as the *Orlando Furioso* is a heroic poem, which Giraldi defines as the imitation of illustrious actions of one or more noble and illustrious men. Of primary consideration, therefore, is the fable, which must be founded on one or more illustrious actions and must be a subject that can be rendered as a poem; i.e., it must have the potential of "ornament" and splendor and be rendered in verse. Giraldi devotes much of the *Discourse* to what fits or does not fit the dignity and gravity of the truly heroic. The subject and the way it is rendered are inseparable: The truly artistic heroic poem has unity of tone, a higher unity than that of mere single action.

On this essential point Giraldi was misunderstood by some critics in his time and has been misinterpreted by some in our day. Giraldi, they maintained, set up a distinctly new genre, the *romanzo*, unknown to Aristotle and therefore completely freed from Aristotelian laws, especially that of unity. Torquato Tasso, stout champion of the single-action unity, wrote: "The *romanzo* (so they call the *Furioso* and other poems like it) is of a genre of poetry different from the epic and, because it was unknown to Aristotle, is therefore not bound by the rules which Aristotle gives for the epic" (*Discorsi del poema eroico*, Bk. III). Tasso then proceeds to show that this view is wrong and that the *romanzo* and the heroic poem are of the same genre:

> The *romanzo* and the epic imitate the same actions, namely the illustrious . . . the generous and magnanimous actions of heroes. . . . The *romanzo* and the epic imitate in the same manner; in both the poet is present; events are narrated, not represented as in drama . . . ; both imitate in the same medium, using unadorned verse, i.e., without the bodily rhythm and music associated with tragic and comic verse. . . . From the agreement therefore of the actions imitated and the medium and the mode one concludes that what is called *romanzo* and what is called epic are of the same genre of poetry. (*ibid.*)

Therefore, Tasso insists, the *romanzo* should have the same single-action unity prescribed by Aristotle. With the sole exception of the rule of single-action, the modern heroic poem as described by Giraldi meets all these requirements prescribed by Tasso. The theme of the *Discourse* is how to write a really artistic heroic poem in modern times. Giraldi would surely have agreed with Tasso that the modern heroic poem called the *romanzo* was of the same genre as the ancient epic.

That which distinguishes Giraldi as a critic perhaps more

than anything else is his emancipating statement that there can be a unity not of the Aristotelian type, at least as the *Poetics* was usually interpreted. His exposition of this different kind of unity not only admitted the *Orlando Furioso* to an equal artistic status with the *Aeneid* but also opened the way to future heroic poems such as, for example, *The Faerie Queene*. Beyond the specific genre of the heroic poem, Giraldi's theory also showed the way to dramatic poems of more than one action, such as *King Lear* and *Bartholomew Fair*.

For Giraldi the modern heroic poem is better if written about many actions by one man, or many actions by many men, than about the one or single action of ancient heroic poems. This diversity of actions, he says, "carries with it a unity in variety which is the spice of delight and so allows a large field to the writer to make episodes and pleasing digressions." But there must be a real unity in this variety; "the poet," he says, "ought to be cautious to treat these digressions so that one depends on another and that they are well linked with the parts of the subject which he has set out to tell with a continuous thread." The "digressions" are not really so; the artistic principle is that they are to be integral parts of a whole which is built on a principle different from the single fable.

Giovambattista Giraldi Cinthio
to the much honored
Gentleman and Lord Signor Boniface Ruggieri
Secretary to His Excellency the Duke of Ferrara

For many years, Signor Boniface, I have thought much about the manner of composing various kinds of poetry. Among those with whom I have shared my thoughts, both in teaching and in familiar discourse, to no one have I more liberally and more solicitously revealed my discourses and shown my industry in these matters than to M. Giovambattista Pigna. He has been more attentive to me than any other and has observed more diligently what I discussed with him and taught him concerning all kinds of poetry. Having observed this young man's assiduity and eagerness to learn, I held him as dear as a son. Such has been my affection for him that I have never had a thought or reflected on literature or devoted myself to any composition without sharing it with him as with my own son. During the time I was his teacher, he asked me in his letters to show him how to defend Ariosto from the calumnies against his Romances. So I wrote him a long, full letter dealing with the objections that had been set forth against our excellent poet. Then it seemed to me that he would be pleased if I should assemble in more detail and in order what I had taught him and others about poetry. For his greater satisfaction and fuller understanding, I resolved to set down in an organized discourse all that I had discussed with him in various ways and at various times about the composition of Romances and other poems.

To this discourse I devoted what time I could take from my many affairs, public and private, and carried it out to completion. Then I gave it to Pigna himself, for since I had composed it expressly for him, it seemed to me I should give it to him first rather than to another. Now that for many years it has been in his possession and in mine, other young men have asked me to make this work available to them also, for although they had heard me speak of the same things, they could not remember them so well, not being able to read and ponder them. Hence I, who am always eager to please insofar as I can, seeing that I could please many with one piece of work, therefore resolved to publish my discourse. Since it was composed for the dearest pupil I had, I have decided to dedicate it to Your Lordship as one of my dearest and most honored friends, because of the rare qualities I have so long known and revered, especially when we went together to Venice as members of the legation on which His Excellency was pleased to send us. In this legation I saw mingled in Your Lordship such nobility of mind and of blood that I noted your excellent traits were not less than the gifts of fortune. Because of your courtesy and other qualities, I came to love and honor Your Lordship much more than before.

Accordingly, Signor Boniface, be pleased to receive this my little gift with the affection with which I offer it to you. I trust that the feeling with which I offer it may compensate to Your Lordship for any defect to be found in it. I kiss your hands and ask your favor.

In setting out to write about the art of composing Romances, Messer Giovambattista, I see I am undertaking a hard and fatiguing task, since, indeed, no one that I am aware of has written on this subject and since many authors have written variously in this form of poetry, not only in other nations and peoples but also among us Italians. My difficulty is increased by your ability and learning, which is such that I doubt my being able to write anything you have not already seen and considered, because, while my pupil, you studied poetry, diligently absorbed what I said, and wrote about poems of all kinds. Since then you have devoted yourself to study and writing and have continually read or written excellent works. But although my undertaking may be difficult and laborious, nevertheless the love I have had for you during the long time you were my pupil leads me to devote myself to the task.

My regard has indeed grown greater as you have continued to go ahead in your studies. This causes me to congratulate myself for the efforts I made for you while you were in my charge more than for those I made for any other pupil. Even though many of my pupils have succeeded notably, no one more than you has joined the serious with other delightful studies. Walking felicitously in my footsteps, not neglecting your major studies, you have also shown the strength of your natural talents in those that are delightfully sweet. For this reason you have become dearer to me day by day. In you more than in any other, it seems I, though grown old, regain my youth. And if indeed I am aware of not now having the powers to set down all that ought to be said about this matter, nevertheless I shall rejoice that this testimony of my love may remain with you. Furthermore, the little I shall treat of now may wake some happy genius to accomplish that which I failed to do and, by lighting a great light from a tiny spark, will illumine the darkness that until now surrounds this mode of composition. For up to this time many writers of Romances have written more often by natural practice than by art. And the benefits that will arise from the discussion of such things makes me hope that out of it may arise such able writers that I shall be among them as a tiny flame is to the sun.

Perhaps I myself, having at some later time more leisure and peace of mind than I now have, may complete with greater diligence what now remains imperfect. In truth I am so occupied with many pursuits—both my private affairs, my domestic duties, the load of public affairs that I bear in the service of my illustrious and excellent master, and my function as public lecturer—that if it were not for gratifying you, I would rather put myself to doing anything else than this heavy task. I hope, however, you may wish me a little more diligence so that at the least I may not seem to be lacking in—I shall not say, common friendship—but rather that love which has always made me hold you no less dear than if you were my son.

In writing what you have asked of me, I shall make no effort to show whether it is better in our times to write in Latin or in the vulgar. Perhaps Bembo[1] and Alessandro Citolini[2] have abundantly resolved that question. Nor shall I undertake to show the necessity of knowledge of philosophy and of all those other arts and disciplines that your own range of knowledge includes. These things, however, are so necessary to good writing that without them one cannot create anything worthy of being read. Nevertheless so much have the Greeks, the Latins, and our Italian authors of today written of them that, it seems to me, to try to add anything to what is already written would be like carrying firewood into a forest. Nor shall I speak here of all that Aristotle wrote in his *Poetics*, which has been made so happily clear in the public lectures of our mutual friend Vincentio Maggio,[3] who is especially excellent in this subject as in all others belonging to rare philosophy, since it seems to me enough has been said about these matters in my *Poetics*.[4]

Having to speak just now on only one subject, namely, the composition of Romances, I shall only pray that I may be alert to this subject and to the gratifying of your demand. But before we proceed further, we should seek to discover what this term Romance signifies and at the same time to study its mode of composition and its relation to Greek and Latin poetry; then we should show why these poems are divided into cantos; finally, we should determine what mode in composing verses ought to be maintained by one who wishes to achieve excellence in this kind of poetry with respect to invention or subject, to the arrangement of parts, to the diction and style, and to its other important aspects.

As to the name, this is the first topic we have proposed. I believe that this name of Romance (besides the other derivations I have discussed with you at length on other occasions when we happened to converse of such matters) came from the term Ρώμη, which in Greek signifies strength; but some Latins prefer to derive it from the word *Roma*, because of the immense strength of the Roman people, *The Name Romance* and also from the name of those who among the Romans were called Ramnes, a word that some have said is derived from Roma, others from Romulus, as the Tatiensi from Tatius and the Lucensi from Lucumone. But leaving this question to those who search into Roman antiquities and remaining of that opinion which seems to me better than all others, I judge that one should not speak of works of Romance but of poems and compositions about the brave knights.

This same term may signify for us the heroic composition as it does for the Latins, although there is one who would derive this word from Remensi, others from Turpin, who in their opinion more than anyone gave material to such poems with his writings. Since he was Archbishop of Rheims (Remense), they maintain that these compositions have been called Romances. And I am easily persuaded that this mode of composing Romances has for us taken the place of the heroic poems of the Greeks and the Latins. Just as those poets in their languages wrote of the illustrious and renowned deeds of the brave knights, so those who have devoted themselves to writing Romances treat with feigned materials of knights whom they call errant. In their compositions are seen virtuous and courageous deeds, mingled with love affairs, with acts of courtesy, with games, with strange events in the manner of the Greeks and the Latins in their compositions.

It seems to me it can be said that this kind of poetry had its origin from the French, from whom perhaps it also had its name. Since in their language are many Greek words, these perhaps may have been used also by those Druids who in France (as Caesar informs us[5]) spoke the Greek language. From the French, then, this manner of writing poetry was passed to the Spaniards, and finally was received by the Italians, whose better authors, unlike those of other nations, have written these works not in prose but in verse and have divided them not into books but into cantos. It may happen that some have divided their works into both cantos and books, others into books only; but I am speaking of the better and more judicious who have made their divisions into cantos only.

Nor did this name canto, given to such poems, originate among us so that through the piazzas and public places these compositions might be sung among the benches in the manner of those nowadays who with lyre on arm sing their idle nonsense to earn their bread; this name had a higher and more honorable origin. Among the Greeks and the Latins (as the writers of both testify, especially Cicero in his book of famous orators[6] and in the fourth of his *Tusculan Disputations*,[7] and, following him, Valerius Maximus, where he discusses the ancient institutions),[8] it was the custom to sing at banquets and dinner tables, accompanied by the lyre, of the glorious deeds of the great masters and of the mighty exploits of virtuous and brave men. So the Italians, following this ancient custom (I speak of the better poets), have ever feigned to sing their poems before princes and noble company. This custom so developed among the Greeks that their singers, called rhapsodes, did not otherwise divide the Homeric poems—according to some, to make them suitable for singing, as the theatrical poets made their plots into acts, or perhaps as our poets made their Romances into cantos.*

Origin of the Canto

---

* Giraldi's longer marginal notes are given in the Appendix, pages 167-80.

From this Greek and Latin usage, then, our Italian poets have drawn their division into cantos, not from the singing of those plebeians who with their nonsense spread their nets for the purses of whoever would listen to them. And each canto is bound by the limit of what can be spoken conveniently at one time and what will without boredom hold the attention of those to whom the poets feign to direct their discourses. Our poets who have thus divided their compositions frequently intended them to speak to those persons before whom they feign to sing. This practice would not be suitable for the Greek and the Latin and for the vulgar poets who would compose in the manner of Vergil and Homer, since they themselves are the narrators and do not have this characteristic, except in introducing the one narrating his own wanderings or his own deeds or those of others, as is seen in Homer's Ulysses and Vergil's Aeneas. But for now, that is enough of this discussion of the name of Romances, their origin, and the division of the poems into cantos.

It remains for us to speak of the mode of composing them and to show what is to be considered and observed in such writing. Since it would take too long to try to explain all that could be considered in this part (let us set aside those matters which serve for examples of ancient writing, referring to what I have written elsewhere on the works of these poets), for the present I shall touch on that which seems to me more necessary and pertinent to the satisfying of what you have asked me regarding the writers of Romances.

The first consideration, then, of one who would devote himself to composing in this form of poetry is the subject or the fable or the matter (as we wish to call it) with which the poet is to work. For above everything else the poet should have prepared the matter on which he may afterward use the powers of his genius.† In the composition of Romances the fable should be founded upon one or more illustrious actions, which the poet may imitate suitably with pleasant language, to teach men honest life and good customs, which should be the foremost end of composing for any good poet. To that end Aristotle believed that the fable is the most essential part to be considered by the poet, indeed to be considered above anything else.⁹

The Subject

The material which the talented man uses and the art with which he writes being, then, of greatest importance, he ought to exercise the utmost care in choosing the material with which a writer may work laudably, such as has the potential of ornament and splendor, such as can be pleasing and useful to one who will devote himself to reading his composition. One who does not do this would, first of all, show little judgment in his choice and then would lose his labor, just as one who tills barren ground gathers no fruit and finds in the end that he has toiled in vain; this would happen likewise to one who would put his study and talent into dealing with material so arid and sterile in itself that it would not be fit to receive any ornament.‡ Indeed, in this matter, it seems to me, Count Matheo Maria Boiardo and our Ariosto were very prudent and farseeing. The former was a very pleasing and noble inventor; the latter, who created his material in such a way that after his invention his work was received by the world as marvelously delightful, was an imitator worthy of the greatest praise. These two are leaders in their achievements. Those who out of feigned materials would write well in such poetry ought to follow in their footsteps with all diligence. Although those who wrote before them may have shown some talent and dealt with many similar matters, as can be seen by anyone who has the leisure to read them, nevertheless all of them have written inattentively of their materials. Yet it may have appeared to some that Luigi Pulci in his *Morgante* was worthy of praise, allowing themselves to be deceived by those ridiculous little Tuscan *novelle* (in which not infrequently indeed there are as many Florentines as Greeks)§ from his Margute (a name perhaps taken from Homer's *Margites*, which was written to be ridiculous) and from other sayings which, however immediately admirable, are rather jokes than works worthy of heroic gravity. Up to now, of those who have written since these two, I have yet to see anyone worthy of the praise that ought to go to a poet who writes notably in this material. And although Boiardo, because of the imperfection of the age in which he was born, did not set down his ideas on paper with such felicity of style and refinement of diction as Ariosto wrote (who in his time truly had many graces that may be seen in the better form of writing),¶ there are in Boiardo many other good qualities that compensate in part for this defect.

In the writing of Romances, the poet's first consideration, then, is the subject, which is to be drawn from his invention. Because heroic poetry is none other than imitation of illustrious actions, the subject of such compositions will be one or more illustrious actions of one or more noble and excellent men; these the poet will imitate pleasingly in language metrically arranged. And because I have said one or more illustrious actions of one or more noble and excellent men, I shall make clear below what I mean. Nor ought the subject alone to be considered and selected from others; great heed should also be accorded to those qualities which, beyond the value that the subject carries in itself, enable the poet to embellish it and to make it pleasing to every kind of person. This our two poets whom we discussed did artfully; besides, having chosen actions illustrious and appropriate to honest customs, they gave to their compositions a general embellishment which makes them pleasing to all readers. Besides the other common and pleasing things dispersed throughout their works, there were religion and the origin of the battles between the Christians and their enemies. This holds one's attention marvelously and makes the reader cheerful about the happy events of those who are of the same faith as he, and sorrowful over the adverse events. Throughout, his mind remains in suspense as he awaits for God to provide relief from the adversities and injuries suffered at the hands of the infidels. There is also much that is appropriate to the terrible and the pitiable, though these two things do not hold the supreme place in such works.

Now in turning to the subject: It should be pointed out that subjects or materials of Romances are not in the manner of Vergil's and Homer's, both of whom undertook imitating only one action of one man, whereas ours have imitated many actions not of one man only but of many, since they build the whole fabric of their work upon eight or ten persons, but they give to the work the name of that person or that action which is dominant in the whole *Romances Not of On Action* work and on which all the others depend, or at least to that which reasonably binds them together. This kind of poem, moreover, came from neither the Greeks nor the Latins; indeed it came laudably from our own language, having given to the excellent writers of it the same authority which the two writers already named gave to their works.

Feigned Subjects Since it is clear that the good authors who have written Romances in this language have feigned their materials and basing themselves on these, have built the edifice of their poetry, it is possible to doubt that in such forms of poetry it was permissible to adhere to ancient subject matter and to found poems on it. To this objection I respond that the newness of the subject doubtless carries with it much charm and much delight, as Aristotle showed in his *Poetics* when he spoke of tragedy, which, as respects imitation of illustrious action, is most like heroic poems. Giving as example *The Flower of Agathon*, he shows that feigned fables are more pleasing because they are not known. Reasoning about this, he shows that in every way it is so, since of the known fables those less known prove more pleasing.[10] Therefore I, not caring what the slanderers may say, composed most of my tragedies from new subject matter I found; yet not to invite comparison with either the Greek or Latin poems that are read today; desiring rather to err with the judgment of Aristotle** than to please those whom nothing pleases except what they themselves do or what conforms to their discourses, often contrary to all sound judgments.

But for all that, I would not censure the authors of Romances who worked with ancient material and handled it well in their poems. Indeed if we see in those poems in which the subjects are feigned that the materials drawn from the ancients have become new, as comparisons, similitudes, metaphors, descriptions of places, of tempests, of battles, and of like things, why do we wish to believe that one ought to be blamed if he deals with subject matter of an ancient mode but merged with new feigned material found by the poets of our time? And if one should say to me that ancient materials are not suitable to be woven into the form of the newly feigned, I reply that experience will show the opposite—when a good poet will appear to deal with ancient subject matter in the form of Romances and to give it that same form of cantos which the writers of Romances have given to their works.

I understand that many noble spirits are now working, who, out of patience with the Orlandos, the Rinaldos, and other like subjects—already too common—have put forward Greek and Latin subjects in which they show most admirably the power of their genius. Nor indeed have they taken one action only but more than one, imitating those many among the Greeks who wrote of the deeds of Bacchus (called Grandfather, which is still the usage in the Greek language), of Hercules, and of Theseus. These writers set out the entire life of one or the other no less artistically than learnedly; yet their works, like those of many others, have been lost in the ravages of time. Vergil, it seems, alluded to such works when he said in his *Georgics*:

> Quis aut Euristea durum,
> Aut illaudati nescit Busiridis aras?
> Cui non notus Hylas puer?[11]

Vergil did not attempt these, since in his time they became no less common than are the creations today about Orlando,

Rinaldo, and others like them. These have indeed become so vulgar that even slipper makers try to write them. Although it is clear that Aristotle in his *Poetics* censures those who devoted themselves to writing the *Theseid* or the *Heracleid*, he does not condemn them (if his words are well considered) for the composition or for the subject, but only because those authors whom he condemns thought that writing the deeds of only one man would make a poem of one action,[12] a view surely far from the truth and worthy of censure.

To conclude this part: The subject then may be of one action or of more, of many men or of one man; the poet ought to be concerned that it be such as can be treated well and be capable of poetic ornaments so that it can ever please not only the learned men but all men of the language in which he writes. Homer so aimed at this in order that all Greece might take pleasure in and profit from his poems, that he employed words common to all the good dialects of Greece in his time, as Plutarch most judiciously writes, who also shows abundantly that the composition of the poet should be legendary, yet with material drawn from history, since without the fable the poem would be without merit.[13] The poem, as he says, is the condiment with which the poet enters stealthily into the mind of him who reads or listens. Joining the useful with the delightful, he offers marvelous cheer, and by the great knowledge of a lively genius, many profitable things to him who reads. It has come about, as said Maximus Tyrius,[14] that the same profit as comes from philosophy has come to men from poetry; that poetry and philosophy differ only in name, but in substance are the same thing; and that the former, under the veil of fable, taught the honest and praiseworthy life, the latter with more open demonstration. By this reasoning he thus puts poetry before philosophy, of which matter we have spoken abundantly elsewhere.

But first let me move on to the other matters in order to indicate more easily what I have to say. Following Plato and the imitation of him by Cicero, I should like to show by similitude the whole fabric of composition which the poet of Romances ought to write. By that fabric I mean the order and texture of the whole work, until it is managed with proper means, to the proposed end.

The similitude is, it seems to me, that the bodies of poems can be likened to the composition of the human body. For as man is made of mind and body, and the body of bones, sinews, flesh, and skin (I wish at present to set aside the other parts of the body which do not fit this proposition), so the compositions of good poets who write Romances ought to have parts of their bodies which correspond to the parts which compose man. *A Poem like a Living Body*

The subject, as we have already said, will hold the same place in the body of the poem as do bones for the man. As the bones sustain all the other parts that compose the man, so the subject is the foundation of the whole work; if this is removed, everything must fall in ruins; it is not enough for the makeup of a man that the bones be beautiful and fit in their composition if they do not have good order and precise proportion; they must be not only well disposed but also tied and joined in such a way that they do not move from their appointed places, but stay in their natural place; therefore the sinews, with their junctures and ligatures, are needed to hold the bones together. Thus the poem needs an order of parts and of ligaments that hold it together. Since, however, to see bare bones, though joined in order, without any ornament is displeasing (as is certified by the images of the dead which we see depicted, and also by those bones of the human body which my dear pupil Battista Canani,[15] excellent master of anatomy, has for many years joined together with wonderful mastery), nature has painstakingly and sagely superimposed on the bones the flesh, which fills in the hollows and smooths the rough places with beautiful and pleasing proportion. But since the flesh in itself, because of its sanguineness, is a noisome rather than a pleasing sight, nature has placed over it the skin, soft, delicate, strewn with a sweet and changing variety of colors, a coverlet that makes the whole composition of the body appear pleasing to whoever admires it. To this body, so well designed and diligently formed, is added the soul, which gives it life, so that the whole fabric of the man is perfected and living.

By this similitude, then, the poet of Romances ought to compose his poem almost as if he would strive to form a living image disclosed as pleasing, graceful, and beautiful. After the poet has found the subject, which we have likened to the bones (although it is clear that for Aristotle the fable, which he takes as the subject, is the soul of the poem;[16] nevertheless at this point I take it in a sense different from his in order to liken it to the bones, in that the subject or fable is the support of the work), he ought to take great care and study diligently the disposition, which in the poem has the same place as the sinews and ligaments of the body. The disposition in itself produces not only the order of the parts but also the connections with which each part is joined to another, if it is composed wisely; and indeed it not only has this in itself but also has those things that fill out, like the flesh from which comes the proportion of the members.

But the first thing to be advised about the disposition (we shall discuss its other aspects as the course of the work will demand) is to know that a subject, dignified, pleasing, noble, and fit to receive splendor and ornament from the poet's efforts, has been found. From this he ought to begin to put the work in order. According to Horace's precept[17] he composes with little art if, after he has chosen a subject to work on, he begins the work from the beginning of what he proposes to write, just as it would be if one should wish to write about what Achilles did at Troy and should begin with the egg of Leda from which Helen was born and trace all that happened from that point to the ruins of Troy. Indeed, according to his statement, it seems better to begin in the midst, then to bring in the other parts as the work proceeds, instead of ornaments. Vergil thus created marvelously in his *Aeneid;* wishing to bring Aeneas into Italy, he began not with the fall of Troy but rather after the city had fallen and after Aeneas had departed; he put the beginning of his poem at Aeneas' departure from Sicily and then had him relate to Dido what had happened to him in the ruins of Troy and, at the same time, all his wanderings.

All this was in imitation of Homer, who did the same in the *Odyssey* regarding Ulysses' wanderings, which were narrated at Alcinous' banquet. I said that Vergil imitated Homer, since, it seems to me, in his *Aeneid* he set out to encompass with a beautiful imitation—insofar as this fit his design—what Homer had written in the *Odyssey* and the *Iliad*. So the first six books of Vergil's *Aeneid* are proportioned to the twenty-four of the *Odyssey;* the other six to the twenty-four of the *Iliad*; thus I am easily led to believe that the *Aeneid* was perfected in that number of books and that it would have been superfluous to add other books to his twelve.

But to come back to where we left off, I say that the components of a poem of one action are to accord with Horace's precept, who said: "Nec gemino bellum Troianum orditur ab ovo."[18] This precept Horace took from Aristotle's *Poetics* and from the example of good poets who devoted themselves to writing poems of only one action.[19]

The Natural Order

If a good poet set out to write about the deeds of Hercules or of Theseus (as many among the ancients did), writing their deeds and their lives (as Pausanias in his *Attica*[20] and elsewhere in many places), and set out in a single poem to write of their whole life, with all the illustrious actions of one or the other in order to put before the eyes of whoever reads an honorable and laudable life of a valorous man—as Xenophon did for Cyrus in his *Cyropedia* and as perhaps Statius intended to do in his *Achilliad* and Silius Italicus[21] did for Hannibal—I do not believe it would be unfitting to start at the very beginning of their life and follow through to the end, because this would not be done without splendor of composition and without pleasure and profit to whoever should read it. If one reads voluntarily in prose the life of Themistocles, Coriolanus, Romulus, Theseus, and other excellent men, why would it be less pleasing and profitable to read about them in verse composed by a good and wise poet who knows how to write the lives of the heroes as a model for the world in verse in the guise of history? I believe that Suidas had such a poem in mind when he said the epic (which is none other than heroic composition in verse) was history. He did not consider it unfitting to set forth in verse, in the manner of history, the life of anyone who merited the name of hero.

As historical composition starts with the beginnings of things, so compositions on the actions of a man's whole life originate from the beginning of his illustrious deeds. If in the cradle he showed sign of his greatness, from the cradle the actions of his life should begin. And if one should say to me that neither Vergil's treating of Aeneas nor Homer's of Achilles in the *Iliad* and of Ulysses in the *Odyssey* did so, it seems to me fitting to answer that both had in mind poems of only one action and not poems that follow the style and manner of history. And although Aristotle thought that whoever devoted himself to such a work would create it without limits and therefore not artistically, it does not seem (I say it with all the respect I have for so great a writer) that this is sufficient reason to deter a judicious poet from understaking such a work.

There are a thousand ways to curtail the length of a work without giving up the depiction of all the life of the one whom the poet has chosen to write about; for example, some things may be predicted by soothsayers, other things may be shown in paintings, still others may be narrated. These are things not of such splendor that they deserve, like the others, to be described at length. In these and similar ways the poet will proceed in such a way that the work will not exceed its due bounds. For the poet ought not to set down everything so fully on paper that nothing remains on which the reader needs to linger and exert a little effort to understand it. In his *Metamorphoses*, Ovid has shown what is fitting for the ingenious poet to do, for abandoning Aristotle's laws of art with admirable mastery, he commenced the work at the beginning of the world and treated in marvelous sequence a great variety of matters; nevertheless he managed to do so in a fewer number of books than Homer did in the *Iliad* and the *Odyssey*, even though both of these embrace a single action. Not unlike Ovid was Pisander among the Greeks in treating a diversity of matters, since he also began his work with the nuptials of Juno and Jove and proceeded to write about all that happened up to his own time. This shows that the laws given by Aristotle apply only to poems of a single action and that all poetical compositions that contain deeds of heroes are not bound by the limits that Aristotle set for poets who write poems of a single action.

Therefore as to the arrangement, which consists entirely in the order, a single precept cannot be given (as regards the beginning of the work); first to be considered, however, is whether one wishes to write a poem of a single action, or of many actions by many men, or of all the deeds of a single man. If we may undertake the first (the single action), it is praiseworthy to follow the example of the writers who wrote admirably of one action, on whom Aristotle and Horace founded their precepts.

The first thing to be observed is not to start at the beginning but at that part which will appear in keeping with the design of the writer, bringing in the other parts by embellishment and for the perfection of the story, as did Homer, who began the *Iliad* not with the beginning of the Trojan war but with the wrath of Achilles, which occurred in the ninth year after the beginning of the contest between Achilles and Agamemnon over Briseis. Plutarch shows that the reason, as he says, was that before the wrath of Achilles nothing memorable had happened between the Greeks and Trojans, since the Trojans, fearing Achilles, had not dared to sally outside the walls; but when Achilles left the battle, Hector came forth and did marvelous deeds against the Greeks. Dares Phrygius and Dictys Cretensis show clearly that this view is not true; but allowing freedom of judgment to everyone, Dio Chrysostom, the excellent philosopher, censures Homer for not starting at the beginning and describing the ruin of Troy from the origin of the war.[22]

Since I have yet to see in our language a poem of this sort of composition which merits praise, I shall not dwell longer on this matter or on its other characteristics (leaving it to the care of whoever wishes to deal with it) but shall see if it will be fitting in our language to admit poetry of this kind, and, when admitted, to inquire into what doctrine ought to be followed, Dio's or Aristotle's, then to consider maturely what one must observe in order to write the kind of composition that can at the same time delight and please—something that I have not yet seen done by anyone who has tried to enter this field.

If the subject of the work is to be of many and varied actions by many and various men, as are the parts (components) of the Romances of our language—as we have shown above—it will begin with the matter of greatest import, with what all the other matters will be seen to depend on, or take their origin from, as we note Boiardo

The Principle of Multiple Unity

and Ariosto have done. Here it is observed that Ariosto, though he begins his work with Orlando and ends it with Ruggiero, does not deserve the blame that some have accorded him, since he adapts himself to the behest of the events he has designed. As Ruggiero was last in the arrangement, so his victory (in accord with the writer's intention) concluded the whole work admirably.

If a subject is taken which deals with the entire life of a man, the poet should first see what sort of man he is whose actions the poet has planned to imitate. If he be such that the beginning of his life carries with it splendor corresponding to his other actions, not only would I not censure one who should set out to write the beginning of his hero's life, but rather I would maintain that he would commit a great fault if he passed over it; for if anyone writes of the deeds of Hercules he should not omit Hercules' boyhood, which perhaps was greater and more honorable than the mature age of many other brave knights.

But if the beginnings of the lives of those they write about are such that these cannot be treated commendably, the writer would show good judgment in passing over them in silence and entering on the undertaking worthy of being sung by a good poet. This the Italian writers of the Romances have done, for although they have had many actions of their knights to relate, they have not begun (I mean poets who are not unworthy of the name) with the deeds of the heroes' childhood but with the splendid actions of their maturity; sometimes, however, the early age and births of knights are narrated either by means of unexpected events or by a person suitably introduced into the poem for this purpose, or through some unprepared-for happening.

Before I proceed to other matters about the arrangement, I want you to know, Messer Giovambattista, that, in my opinion, if one is to write on ancient material in the form of Romances, it is better to choose many actions of one man than one action only, since, it seems to me, this method is more suited to composition in the form of Romances than is one sole action. I say this because diversity of actions carries with it the variety that is the spice of delight and so allows the writer a large field to use episodes, that is, pleasing digressions, and to bring in events that can never, without risk of censure, be brought into poems of a single action (I am, however, referring to compositions in this language and to those works that we are now discussing). The poet ought to be careful to treat these digressions so that one depends on another and so that they are well linked with the parts of the material which with a continuous thread and with a continuous chain he has set out to tell, and so that they convey verisimilitude so far as it belongs to poetic fictions, as we shall demonstrate below in the proper place. If these digressions should be made otherwise, the poem would become defective and tedious, just as it delights and pleases when these originate in such a way that they appear to be born with the chief subject.

Multiple Action Preferred

Organic Interrelation of Parts But, returning to our subject: When the writer has planned where he is to begin his work, he ought to exercise great diligence to see that the parts fit together as do the parts of the body, as noted above. In putting the framework together, he will seek to fill up the hollows and to equalize the size of the members. This can be done by putting the filling matters in proper and necessary places, such as loves, hates, plaints, laughter, jests, grave matter, discords, peacemakings, ugly and beautiful things, descriptions of places, times, persons, fables feigned by himself and drawn from olden times, voyages, wanderings, shows, unforeseen events, deaths, funeral rites, lamentations, recognitions, things terrible and pitiable, nuptials, births, victories, triumphs, single combats, jousts, tournaments, catalogs, marshaling of troops, and other similar things which perhaps are such that it would be no small task to detail all one by one. There is nothing above or under the heavens or in the depths of the abyss that is not at the command and under the judgment of the prudent poet who can with varied ornaments embellish the body of his work and bring it not merely to an excellent but to a lovely figure. With these he gives the parts a just measure and decorous ornament, in such proportion that the result is a disciplined and well constituted body.

The arrangement ought to be considered not only in the principal parts, which are the beginning, the middle, and the end, but in every bit of these parts. For this reason the poet ought to consider not only the whole body but each particular part, so that each may be set with beautiful order in its place, with admirable grace, and with the proper proportion and so that the whole, with that beauty and grace, will be to each of them proper and fitting. Just as the face takes on its own beauty and color and as the neck takes both in another form, and the breast, the arms, and the other parts of the body have their own forms, so the ornaments of each part of the poem are varied and diverse. Concerning this matter it is not possible to give laws other than to advise the writer that he discern in the light of his judgment what belongs to the form of the body on which he is about to create, advising him, however, not to become so preoccupied with one part that it makes the others, by not fitting in the whole, seem ugly or their beauty deformed. It is better that the whole be moderately beautiful than that two or three be so excellent that their excellence both to themselves and to the others be a cause of the deformity of the rest—a fault which it seems Sannazaro noted in certain places in Ariosto. But it is evident also in Claudian among the Latins in his *Panegyrics*, in which are to be observed some excellent parts, others less than moderately to be commended. I do not, however, say this because I do not know that among the heroic poets are found the grand style, the low, and the middle, that are dissimilar in themselves; but I say it because in any sort of style the tone suited to it should be kept.††

How to Learn Judgment

Since I have said that in literary composition the light of judgment ought to be the guide, let me say that this judgment is acquired in two ways: first, by conversing and discussing with men learned and used to composing. To a man not of dull or of weak intellectual capacity, one day's conversation with a man who is learned, prudent, and expert in composing and who will talk of things related to it will do more than a year's study—so great is the force of the living voice of him in whom he who would succeed in this discipline trusts as the model from whom he would learn. It should be pointed out that it is not enough that he who speaks explain and teach faithfully but it is necessary also that he who listens be able to adapt himself to learning, to set aside an arrogant manner and the belief (which is the mortal poison of him who thinks he knows a great deal) that he needs no teacher. Such individuals frequently remain in an elementary state or are enveloped in a thousand errors which fill them with distorted and perplexed conceits, afterward expressed so tortuously that they seem as drunkards talking in the madness of wine that takes away their sense, for even if Bacchus were among the Muses, it is much better to get pure conceits with the pure waters of Castalia and Aganippe and to express these simply and gracefully. If the poet lets Bacchus take away his brains, he will then write like a madman and cause all the world to laugh, since what to him seems marvelous, because of his notion, moves laughter in those who know what a good and regular composition ought to have.

He who learns ought to exercise the greatest care not to come upon a man of wrong judgment whose ability (as I am accustomed to say) turns backward, as some I have known who are regarded as learned, to whom, nevertheless, everything has been pleasing except that which is praiseworthy. Those young men can truly be said to be unfortunate who, in their bad luck, come upon such brains for which everything is stinking except what conforms to their twisted and corrupted judgment, and who always teach what cannot be unlearned without the greatest effort.

The other way to acquire judgment is to read and observe

diligently the writings of those authors who have attained excellence in this form of poetry and to discern their excellencies, seeking with all zeal to emulate them. Anyone doing so will not only form his judgment but will also be stimulated to exercise it in composing. Often the same spirit that inspired the poet whom he reads will work also in him and will kindle in him flames which will little by little set his spirit afire and fill it with the same frenzy the Greeks called enthusiasm,‡‡ by which he, as though touched by a stinging inspiration, will be as though he were driven to set forth on paper those things born in his mind through the reading of his author. This has happened to me many times, and I believe, Messer Giovambattista, that you have had similar experience. When I have had in mind nothing to compose, I have, by reading some poet, been constrained, as though despite myself, to grasp a pen and to write the ideas that came into my mind. This I believe comes about through what our minds naturally have in common to receive that inspiration of which we spoke. Filled with the seed of those things suited to harmony and the poetic spirit, as soon as they are helped, our minds produce their fruits. Or this is what happens because, as Aristotle says, poetry is natural to man, and our minds are readily moved by that to which nature itself calls them.

The judicious reader ought to exercise the greatest care to avoid the vices of those whom he reads and to emulate only the virtues, for even in good writers are found those things that ought to be avoided rather than followed. These are mixed with those full of excellence and, if not foreseen, enter stealthily into one's mind and sometimes

Indecorum in Some Great Poets

through the imperfection of our nature, which easily tends toward the imperfect, have more potency than the virtues. These same vices proceed for the most part either from the place where the poets were born or from the age in which the good poets whom we read wrote, or from the nature of the poet. Vergil, being too modest—often in amorous things—failed of that pleasing lasciviousness which was excessive in Ovid, for he was of another nature than Vergil. And great Homer, because he was born in a Greece abounding in vices and because he had a nature prone to wine, spoke of it perhaps more often than may be fitting in a prudent poet.§§ Likewise because of the age in which he wrote, he sowed among the splendors of his poems many things that were censurable in following ages.¶¶ That these were vices of Homer's age and the following ages, and not of the poet, Euripides also shows in his tragedies, as indeed I wrote to that happy spirit del Poncio[23] in dealing with tragedy.

Similar things are also found in Sophocles, who was of the time of Euripides; and in Aeschylus, who was superior to both, though less cultivated and less judicious. After the time of Aeschylus, therefore, his plays were not acceptable nor performed unless corrected. May the Lord grant that this be done also in our time, so that those dramatic works may not be seen which to the great shame of our age are vile and opprobrious and of bad example.

But to lay aside discussion of tragedy, in Homer's *Odyssey* are many similar matters, particularly when he has Nausicaa, the daughter of Alcinous, go to the river with the other young women to wash clothes; this in our time would be unbecoming to a plain workman's daughter, to say nothing of a prince's or a gentleman's daughter. This came about because the poets of those early times accepted a certain rude simplicity of the time far removed from that grandeur, with its regal and reverential display, which appeared later, along with the excellence of imperial Rome. Though this majesty has lost the magnificence of the empire, it has lasted in large measure even to our time. It would be a great error to follow Homer in those things which, though suitable to his time, were inappropriate to the majesty of Rome and likewise to our time. Those who now wish to transfer to their compositions those things which seemed lacking in gravity to Roman judges (especially to the most judicious Vergil, who, almost like a new bee, drank only ambrosia from the native flowers and fields of poesy, seasoning with it his sweet compositions) would incur great censure.

Vergil is the model by which is judged matters dignified and magnificent; human imperfection being such that one man cannot of himself perfectly attain the power of poetically composing great things, nature produced Vergil, who with marvelous judgment devoted himself to creating all the good found in all other Greek and Latin writers, assembled them into one work, to submit to the eyes of those who were to write after him, as the truest example of the composition of heroic grandeur. Vergil was born at the time when the Roman majesty had so risen that it could go no higher; and poetical matters, scattered in the multitude of others' compositions, were such that they only lacked someone to lift them from darkness and make them known when united and disposed marvelously in a very beautiful form. It seems to me that Vergil imitated in this the excellent painters who strove to form a single image

Vergil a Model of Decorum

in representing womanly beauty. They looked at all the beautiful women they could find and from each took as their model the best parts; having assembled as many as seemed sufficient to complete the idea they had in mind, they devoted themselves afterward to creating the imagined figure. This, being made up of the excellent parts of many beauties,*** turned out not just beautiful but so excellent that no living woman's form could match it, so much the noble artificers desired to achieve the ultimate perfection. And although there are some things even in Vergil which show him to be human, these nevertheless are like little moles in the beautiful face of a great madonna. He would also have removed these if death, jealous of so much greatness, had not broken the thread of his life, so that he would not contain so much of the divine that he would not be held in some part human. Though the age of Homer and the mores of that time and the unique qualities of this divine poet made these things tolerable in him, to do the same things now would be to select from the gold of his work the dross (which came to us not from the poet's imperfection but from the age and time) and yet to think that one had chosen from it the purest gold, as is evident in Trissino's *Italia*.

While Trissino attempted in his poem to imitate the defects not of Homer but of the age in which he wrote (since he thought it sufficient if he expressed them well), and to accept everything that good judges would omit, he reveals himself as one of little dignity. If his judgment had been equal to his knowledge, he would be much more highly regarded than he is now and would perhaps not have said that our Ariosto's *Furioso* (from which he nevertheless borrowed many things and perhaps made them worse) was a vulgar work, as he said of it in this verse of his, like the others, very languid: "With his *Furioso*, which pleases the vulgar."[24] If there is anything in Ariosto (as indeed there is, since I do not wish to deny the truth) that does not attain the final ultimate excellence he was able to reach, nevertheless (as Aristotle says of Homer)[25] the lights of his ability are so many and give off such splendor that those bits which are not in themselves so shining are illuminated by it.

The imperfection of our nature, Messer Giovambattista, and I say it not without sorrow, does not allow anything to come from us, even by the effort that we give it, that is so perfect in every respect that it is not known in the end as coming from a man, and that it is human, not divine. Though good things which heaven can give us mortals are dispersed among men, they are never found in one single man. And they can be called four or six times blessed in whose literary works may be found excellencies that make their defects tolerable—not only tolerable but worthy of pardon. The noble spirit ought not so to fix his eyes on one thing that carries within itself some defect that he cannot see the excellencies that hide this defect under their cloak. He who wishes to take from Homer material to write about ought to stick only to that which fits the age in which he writes, not to seize upon that which, although tolerable in Homer's age for the reasons given, today appears very horrid in the writers who need to be given authority and cannot give it to things that do not have it in themselves.

And perhaps that painter who depicted Homer as vomiting and all the poets as staining their fingers in his vomit and going home,[26] did it with the judgment of a keen spirit who, born in a better time, wished to show by that painting that, although the works of Homer might give material for composing to all poets (as in truth his poems do give to them), not all that Homer wrote is fitting for all times, for all ages, for every condition of person. What was drawn from him needed to be better digested and brought to that perfection which would be entirely consonant with the time in which it was written, so that what was drawn from him would be improved.

Cicero taught us this when he said that the Romans borrowed many things from the Greeks but then made them better. Granted that the compositions of Homer were marvelously praised by the great geniuses of Greece and that they thought that what was in him was laudable, it happened partly because the ambitious Greeks wished to show that their poet was not just excellent but divine; thus they said that his native land was heaven, not those cities about which they disputed as producing him; and partly because their judgment was formed in that nation, in those customs and in that mode of speaking; and the fitness of such things made them judge accordingly. Because they had not seen the method of writing verse that later existed in Vergil's time, they held Homer's verse to be the most perfect possible, as happened among the Latins regarding Ennius, who, however rudely he wrote, was nevertheless considered even in Cicero's time an excellent poet. But when Vergil arrived, Ennius had no value. So great was the Roman judgment when the grandeur of the empire was realized, and especially that of Vergil, and so removed from those Greek ineptnesses in which those minds were immersed that they did not even recognize ineptnesses. Therefore, although in the writings there was poor quality in many places, in their prolific language one does not find (as Cicero says) the word *inept*, although some today show certain Greek words which they say have that meaning. This is, however, as far from true as these words are from giving the force of the word *inept*. Granted that some Greek words are somewhat similar to this one, they do not for all that contain in themselves all that is in this word, as may be clear to whoever will make diligent comparison of them.

But turning to Vergil: It seemed to Tucca and Varius[27] that Vergil was outside the decorum of Roman majesty when Aeneas in the burning of Troy, having seen Helen, kindled to wrath, and driven by madness, tried to kill her. Therefore they omitted from the second book of the *Aeneid* some twenty-two verses relating to this incident.[28] But what would they have thought if Vergil had brought in two kings, two brave captains, to talk insultingly to each other as Homer has his persons to talk? But why do I speak of kings and mortal persons? Their most important gods and goddesses not merely do the same thing but even much worse. I believe (setting aside the ravings of whoever may regard such things as marvels) that they would no more have praised Homer than we would Ariosto if he had put in his poem the faintings of Amadis of Gaul[29] in the fury of the battle when he sees his Oriana, at the sight of whom many times in conflicts his weapons fell from his hand; and because of it, he is as if he were dead, or as if he were a frail little woman or a tender boy. This kind of thing Ariosto never imitates in his Romances, although in some other ways he imitated *Amadis* and other Spanish works. It seemed to Ariosto that, even if perhaps those things were fitting either to the nation or the times in which *Amadis* was written, they did not suit his own times or the people whom he brings into his Romances. Although many say that Homer, under these discussions and those fictions that we say do not belong in our time, deals with mysteries, secrets of nature, and celestial things; these people with their ravings can never bring me to judge it a good thing to become lowly and vile, with a touch of the foolish, in great and heroic poems, by trying to give the gift of prophecy to whoever reads poetic compositions.

The Poet an Artist, Not a Philosopher On the contrary I shall judge that it is more fitting for the good poet to serve decorum and the qualities of things and people and to appear judicious than to try to be a philosopher, to make himself known as of little esteem in that art from which he has his name. Though Aristotle pardons the poet for the errors that do not pertain to his art, if, for example, he errs in building arts, navigation, catching birds, fishing, military tactics, and other similar things; he does not nevertheless pardon in any way commission of errors pertaining to his art.[30] Not departing from the fictions, however, the great Vergil employed them with the manner and the grandeur fitting the dignity of those times, showing how philosophical ideas ought to be introduced into poems by anyone, because while showing himself to be a philosopher he did not fail to make the most excellent of poets.

This I believe Homer also would have done, if the nature of his times would ever have shown them to him. However, we are not without those who, incited to envy because of Vergil's greatness, have tried to show that Vergil does not even come near Homer in greatness. This Macrobius showed politely in the Fifth Book introducting Eustathius (who perhaps was the one who interpreted Homer with such a long exposition), who took the part of Homer, seeking with much zeal to show that Vergil is in large measure inferior to him.³¹ It appears also that Servius in his comment on the *Aeneid* is of this same opinion, unless we allow that a mere grammarian is not qualified to give an opinion on such things.³² Quintilian, not daring otherwise than to give freely of his own opinion, offered us that of Domitius Afer, in an attempt to demonstrate that Vergil was not at all inferior to Homer.³³ Although Pliny says that no poet was more felicitous than Homer,³⁴ this must be understood to mean among Greek poets; if indeed he had intended to understand it also of Vergil, it would not be remarkable if he was deceived, when one considers that he let slip from his pen that Vergil believed the Sandyx was a grass,³⁵ not understanding the meaning of the verse, "Sponte sua Sandix pascentes vestiet agnos."³⁶ In that passage Vergil did not intend to say that the lambs eating the Sandyx will take on its color, but that the fleeces would not need to be colored because, since the lambs pastured on grass, they would acquire their color from nature. Vergil named the Sandyx not because he meant that they would be dyed with that color but only that he took the particular for the universal; it was as though he had said, while the lambs eat the grasses, the fleeces by nature, will be dyed with every color.†††

But to go on now to discuss the disposition or arrangement which we have laid aside for so long: When used with judgment, it bears with it the chain with which one part is joined to another, not unlike the sinews and other ligaments that tie together the parts of the human body. One should take into account that the poems of the Romances have a mode of being linked unlike that of

The Disposition or Arrangement

the heroic poems of the Greeks and Latins, who wrote poems of one action, as did Homer and Vergil and other excellent poets of these two languages, since these poets have joined one book with another with continuous narration by means only of a certain dependence with respect to subject matter. The writers of the Romances who have the highest reputation have not been content only with dependence of one on another but have striven further to put into one canto after another, before they develop a continuation of matter, something to prepare the way for what they intend to say. In this technique Ariosto succeeded marvelously. Yet because there are those who censure him for what seems to me worthy of the greatest praise, that is, the beginnings of his cantos, I think it not remote from my purpose to discuss this and to show how much more praiseworthy it is to prepare the way in such a manner than to accept in this form of poetry the arrangement of Vergil and Homer.

To stress this matter, it will not be amiss for me to go back to what I said previously and to note that these compositions (the Romances) are divided into cantos, for our poets either sing or feign to sing in the presence of great princes, as was the custom of the ancient Greeks and Latins. The reason why they promise at the end of their cantos that they will return to sing and why they feign at the beginning of the cantos that they have returned to sing where they had left off was their need, before resuming the primary material, to get the attention of their hearers. They do this as would a good performer on the lyre or lute or any other similar instrument, who, before he starts to play, takes his instrument in hand and seeks with a few sweeps over the strings to catch the ears of those before whom he is to play. So our poets, seeking from canto to canto renewed attention with some pleasing beginning, arouse the minds of the hearers; and then when the poets come to the continuation of the matter, they link one canto to another with marvelous mastery.

Perhaps our poets took this custom from Claudian, who in many of his *Panegyrics* (almost like the rhapsodies sung at the feasts we spoke of) sets forth some elegies that prepare the way for what he has to say. This he did not only in the *Panegyrics* but in the three books that he composed on the rape of Proserpine; insofar as this was decorous for him, in these last three books one can observe admirably what we mentioned above. There is another difference in linking parts between our poets and the ancient heroic poets. Since the writers of Romances have taken the actions of many men from the beginning, they have not been able to continue one matter completely from canto to canto.

In order to conduct the work to the end, it has rather been their technique, first to speak of one person, then to interpose another by interrupting the first subject and entering upon the deeds of the other, and on this design to continue the matters to the end of the work. This they have done with marvelous art. In their breaking off of one matter for another, they lead the reader by such endings that, before they break off, they leave in his mind an ardent desire to return in order to discover the matter that was broken off. Their whole poem is thus read, since the principal matters are not concluded until the completion of the work. *Narrative Technique of Romances*

If anyone should intend to compose the actions of only

one man, he would be able to continue one canto after another without breaking the theme and without leaving off and then resuming and following it anew. To choose for the foundation of a work only one man and to write of his deeds, it is not necessary to break off the work in order to speak of the actions of another, except insofar as another person must be involved in this same action. Perhaps it is more laudable to compose in this manner than in the first which we mentioned, since that beauty which the writers of such compositions seek to actuate, with the variety of the actions of many men, can in several ways be brought properly into the poem that contains the many actions of one man and thus relieve the reader of the boredom of always reading the same thing. If it should appear to anyone that the matters of the cantos are extensive, I say that whoever will consider well how many times in the other Romances the poets return to interrupted matter before the completion of the work will see that the matters in those works are much longer than in those that go on in cantos and actions with a continuous thread. These can indeed be managed by an ingenious poet (how seldom he has, we said) with marvelous variety. If this came about in Homer and Vergil in writing one action in many books, how much better will it happen to him who will write many actions?

So, Messer Giovambattista, there can occur in their compositions love affairs, unexpected events, acts of courtesy and justice, wrongs, liberality, vices, virtues, offenses, defenses, deceits, infidelities, faithfulness, loyalty, courage, cowardice, hopes, fears, usefulness, injuries, and other such episodes or digressions; and they can bring in, along with the knitting together and disposition of the work, so much variety and delightfulness that the poem will become most pleasing and entertaining without the breaks in the action used by our writers. I do not wish to censure these writers, rather to praise them, since, constrained for the reasons already stated, they cannot do otherwise if they would bring their works to conclusion. If it was lawful for Diodorus Siculus, prose writer, to do this for variety of the subject matter that he undertook to narrate, why should it not be allowed to our poets who write under the more stringent laws in verse?

To speak now generally: I say that judicious authors gifted in composing ought not so to limit their freedom within the bounds set by those who wrote before them that they dare not set foot outside the tracks of others. Apart from being a bad use of the gifts that mother nature gave them, such restraint would prevent poetry from going beyond certain bounds which one writer has marked off and from moving a foot from the way the first fathers made it walk. The great Vergil, understanding that if architecture, military science, rhetoric, geometry, music, and the other arts worthy of the liberal mind are allowed to add, to increase, to diminish, to change, judged that this was much more fitting for the poet, to whom had been given the same power given by the consent of the world to the excellent painter, namely, the authority to vary the likenesses according to the artistic purpose. He showed therefore how in many places good writers, treading where the ancients trod, can turn aside somewhat from the beaten path, letting at times their own footprints go toward Helicon. This is to be seen not only in the Latins but also in the Greeks, above all in Homer, and even more in our Tuscan poets,

Undue Limitation by Ancient Poets

whose compositions are of no less value in their language than those of the Greek and Latin poets in theirs, although the Tuscans have not followed the ways of the Greek and Latin. To speak truly, our language has also its forms of poetry so properly its own that they are not those of any other language or nation. Indeed one ought not to try to hold the Tuscan poet within the confines that bind the Greek and Latin, as we have said sufficiently elsewhere.

Modern Poets as Models One ought to walk along those roads which the better poets of our tongue have laid out, with the same authority that the Greek and Latin poets have had in their languages. For this reason I have laughed many times at some who have wished to proclaim the writers of the Romances to be completely under the laws of art as given by Aristotle and Horace, not considering that neither of them knew this language or this manner of composing. Indeed these works are not to be put at all under such laws and rules, but ought to be left with the boundaries set by those who among us have given authority and reputation to this form of poetry. Just as the Greeks and Latins have drawn the art of their writing from their poets, so we also ought to draw from our poets and hold ourselves to that form which the better poets of the Romances have given us. We see that Ovid, ingenious poet, laid aside in his *Metamorphoses* the laws of Vergil and Homer and did not follow the laws of Aristotle given us in his *Poetics*; nevertheless, he emerged as a beautifully artistic poet, with such benefit to the Latin language that he became a wonder. He was not reprehended nonetheless because he did not follow in the footsteps of the others. This happened because he devoted himself to the writings of matter for which rules and examples did not exist, just as there were no materials on our Romances. Just as he who would write a poem of one action would err if he ignored his models and the laws derived from all the works of like composition, so he who would write Romances of more than one action would err if he did not follow those who are now recognized as great and excellent; in the Romances of more than one action the writers to be followed will be those whose mode of composing will merit praise.

But, not to digress from my first topic: Since in the disposition three things pertaining to the whole are customarily considered in particular, namely, the setting forth of the argument, the invocation, and the narration, these three parts ought to be considered by the poet of Romances. Since these subjects have been written about so copiously by a large number of authors, Greek, Latin, and Italian, to avoid length I shall confine myself to what I have read by the good authors.

I shall say only that the Latin poets practice not putting into the arguments the proper names of those of whom they write, but either indicate them by some names called by the Greek and Latin grammarians as patronymics—as derived from the names of the fathers—or make the names known by circumlocution. The first manner comes from Statius in the *Achilleid*, the second from Vergil in the *Aeneid*, who, having made the first six books similar to Homer's *Odyssey*, intended to follow the beginning of the *Odyssey* in describing Aeneas; rather than use Aeneas' proper name, he gave him a patronym, as Homer did for

Patronyms

Achilles in the *Iliad*. But although the Romances are nearer to the *Odyssey* than to the *Iliad*, they have departed from the model of Vergil and have rather followed Homer in the *Iliad*, putting in the proper names. This has happened because of the variety of the actions of those of whom they wrote; naming them by circumlocution would have created obscurity and confusion. Indeed it was better that they were fitted with their own names. But in the Romances of one action or more, it would be only good (I believe) to follow the custom of Vergil in the *Aeneid*, which he took from Homer's *Odyssey*, if the circumlocution would not perhaps create obscurity or hold the reader's mind too much in suspense or be out of keeping with other things. Otherwise I hold that the proper names should be used.

The Invocation Now as to the invocation, let me say that ever since the emperors subjected Roman liberty, their names began to be invoked as the terrestrial gods, along with the muses and the gods; for this reason they were called august, perhaps because their greatness had persuaded men to regard them as sacred. The Greeks called the emperors σεβαστόι as with this word they intended to show that the emperors were among men as saints and as divine. This was not done in Homer's time, since this greatness was not recognized by men and indeed was not known either by him or by his age. The kings of Homer's time did not command that respect or that reverence which is seen in the Roman emperors and which is continued even to our time (this has increased, if not in dominion, at least in ceremony and in repute). After the poets of the time of the emperors adopted the practice of invoking them in their works (as is seen not only in the poets but also in prose writers as Valerius Maximus), many of them who have written in our language have invoked the princes under whom they have written; and not only the princes but also the chief men of the republics, as Politian did of the Magnifico Lorenzo de' Medici under the name of Lauro in his *Stanze,* which, if I am not mistaken, were the first that proved worthy of praise and carried in themselves spirit and poetic dignity. For them perhaps Politian merited more praise than for the verses he wrote in Latin, in which, though he was equal to, even superior to, his time, he did not have one who in the stanzas of great length could approach him; he far excelled everyone who had written up to his time, accompanying art with nature and thought with choice language. He so survived the age in which he wrote (except that his descriptions and episodes are more diffuse than they ought to be, a fault he perhaps would have corrected if he had finished the work) that he became eminent.

The custom, then, of invoking the princes under whom the poets wrote comes after the subjection of the liberty of the Roman republic. I should like to believe that this custom would have seemed praiseworthy to the ancients if it had been introduced in their time and if there had been poets to give it authority, as the Latins had given it authority in Roman times and the writers of Romances have in our time. Indeed many things which in one time could appear censurable become laudable in another, through usage and authority given to them by whoever was able to do so. Many others which in early times appeared laudable come to be, through change of times, of customs, of human nature, of the heavens, and of adverse regions, either not well thought of or censurable.

I maintain that it is better to follow the usage of the time made reputable by worthy writers than to follow in the steps of those who wrote when such usage had not been introduced. Usage that the age and the time brings to us is of the greatest importance in all the actions of the world.

It should be observed that gods are invoked not only at the beginning of works but also at other places, either for the interpolation of new material or indeed for malevolence coming from the greatness of the matter or from the length of time or from the infinite number or from other conditions; there are examples in Homer, Vergil, and Ariosto himself. It is so frequent in Trissino's *Italia* that it becomes a vice. Granted that at the beginning of the books it is permissible to invoke the emperors or others we have mentioned, this would not be fitting in any of the other parts, as in the catalogs, in the conflicts, and in the other elements placed later in the work, where only the gods are invoked and especially the muses who are believed to favor the poets.‡‡‡ The invocation is made so that the hearer may be attentive, seeing such matter is at hand which could not be carried to completion without divine aid.

The Two Modes of Romances Appertaining also to the composition and to the disposition, one should know that there are two modes of writing Romances: the one which feigns the matter as did Boiardo and Ariosto; the other which chooses matter from antiquity. There are also two modes of treating the materials. Indeed, he who feigns the subject can at will feign and refeign, since he has in hand the whole subject and is not bound by any limits; all depends on his genius and judgment. He who chooses from ancient material is constrained to stay within the limits that he has placed for himself, of necessity, to observe those names, those parts, those qualities without which recognition of the fable would be lost or indeed of the subject that he has undertaken to write.

It is well to point out that although the author or poet who writes of ancient matter is restricted by such necessity, he is not so obliged that he cannot in the course of the work feign new things, as Vergil feigned Laocoon in the ruins of Troy[37] (in this he was imitated by Quintus of Calabria)[38] and the battles of Entellus and Dares in the games of Anchises,[39] and Euryalus and Nisus in the battle of Italy,[40] and the two giants whom Turnus killed.[41] These he nevertheless took from the examples of others, as well as many other things which for brevity I am not mentioning. Not only is this permitted to the heroic poet but so also is the writing of things otherwise than as they are, as did Statius, who put marrow in the lion's bones (in this he was imitated by Ariosto) although the naturalists say that of animal bones the lion's are without marrow. So likewise did Vergil in feigning the stags in Lybia;[42] stags are not found there, although Lybia is full of many other wild animals, as Herodotus testifies.[43] Vergil also brings in the love of Aeneas and Dido, which could not reasonably have occurred, only to show in a poetic fiction that Carthaginians were subjected to Romans, were roused by them to rebel three times, and ultimately were destroyed. So also he feigned Anchises' death in Sicily,[44] whereas the Greek authors had him die and be buried among the Orchomeni in Arcadia. Not only did Vergil feign this, but Ovid also feigned the material in the fable of Numa and Pythagoras,[45] who were of different times though he represented them as being of the same. Catullus likewise feigned in the *Epithalamium of Peleus and Thetis*,[46] making Peleus fall in love with Thetis while Peleus was going to Colchis with the Argonauts, and having the nuptials occur at that time; as a matter of fact, these were celebrated much later, in the time that Priam was king of Troy and Paris was a shepherd on Mount Ida. At these nuptials the three goddesses were rivals for the apple thrown by Discord to be given to the most beautiful, as Coluthus the Theban,[47] among others, shows us where he writes of the rape of Helen. Although some excellent writers are firmly of the opinion that Catullus borrowed the material of this epithalamium, on the contrary he translated it into Latin from the verses in which Hesiod included the same nuptials.§§§[48] But as such a manner is fitting in the episodes or digressions, what we want to say is that it would not fit in with the primary subject, where no authors wrote diversely of the thing, and it was pleasing to the poet to adhere to one more than another; or to choose partly from one and partly from another, as did the better poets of the Greek and Latin language, especially Ovid, who in his *Metamorphoses* relates many things otherwise than the Greek authors did, as in the story of Alcumena he has young Galanthis deceive Juno and then he changed into a stoat or weasel.[49] The Greek writers ascribe this not to Galanthis but to Historide, daughter of Tiresias. Whereas Ovid has Lucina to be the one who impeded her [Alcumena] in the birth, some Greeks say that female magicians did this, commanded by Juno to do so. The same is seen in the fable of Narcissus, in which Ovid (like many others) would have Narcissus enamored of himself and die of it;[50] nevertheless there are those who would have him die because he was in love not with himself but with one of his own sisters, with whom he consummated his passion; when she was dead, Narcissus, going to the fountain, seeing there the image of himself, and remembering his dead sister, took his life because of his great passion for her.

Among the Greeks there are differences also over the battle that Hercules had with King Erginus of the Minyans; some would have it that Erginus was slain by Hercules, others that Hercules came to terms with him and thus did not kill him or chase him from the kingdom. The same is present in the fable of Daphne and Apollo, as told by Ovid;[51] some Greeks maintained that Daphne was not changed into a laurel but was loved by a youth named Leucippus, who despaired of being able to have her for his wife; having no beard and very long hair, he pretended to be a girl and concealed himself among Diana's nymphs. The result was that Apollo, enamored of Daphne, became jealous of Leucippus and induced the girls to bathe in the river Ladone. When Leucippus also entered the river and was known to be a man, the girls with great violence murdered him. The fable of Tantalus was written differently by Philostratus than by Ovid, and differently from both by Atheneus, who has him always with a stone above his head which he will not let go of (for fear of exhausting himself by falling) to taste the appetizing and abundant foods that Jove granted him.[52] Vergil afterward depicted Tantalus, the Lapithae, and others in the sixth of the *Aeneid*.

That essentially the same matter can be written variously may be seen in the writers of tragedy, who treat the same fable in various versions. So there is abundant illustration by those among the Greeks and the Latins who have written of the Argonauts. These, writing variously and preserving the essentials, changed the order and the persons, stressed some details and added others, as it seemed to them fitting to make the poem worthy of praise and in the mode that they planned it to be, to make it expressive of their genius and of nature. He who writes ought not above everything else to depict nature wrongly, and should not be so bound by the laws of others, which would make him a slave and place him completely in their power, that he may never be so bold as to move his feet without the pedagogue who taught him to walk. I say, however, that it seems to me the writer ought not to take so much license that he considers himself to be beyond all rules and freed from all laws, but that he ought to follow the path of others not as a slave but as those who, retaining their own power, will not depart from what is essential to write artistically, as is the custom of good poets.

Since poetry is all imitation, and only the imitation and the verse make the poet; and since the imitation itself, in relation to the subject of the poem, is not about one thing only but about many actions, the poet ought to be most careful that the actions he chooses for his subject and for the foundation of the structure of his work convey in themselves and in the disposition and in the other parts so much verisimilitude that faith is not strained and that one part depends upon another so that necessarily or verisimilarly one comes after the other. He should not do as Trissino did in the fable of Faulo and Ligridonia,[53] which is brought into his *Italia* needlessly and without any dependence. This is one of those episodes or digressions that break the continuity and make the fable faulty; therefore Aristotle censured them drastically.[54] But Trissino, wishing to make use of allegory with this fiction (drawn indeed from others and in part from Ariosto's fable of Alcina and Logistilla),[55] did not look further and was content to show he understood Greek names, even though he fitted the fable neither probably nor necessarily to the continuity, since it broke the necessary sequence, for which the knights enticed by Ligridonia had been sent by Belisario.

The parts and the episodes should, then, have either a necessary or a probable dependence one upon the other. If the work should not be so made, it could little delight or please, which ought to be the principal aim of the poet. If belief in what he writes were taken away, he who reads could not accept it.

Concerning the verisimilar, one should know that not only that which happens probably can be so called but also that which is accepted in the usage of the poets as the verisimilar. Many things in Boiardo, in Ariosto, also in Homer, Vergil, and in Ovid's *Metamorphoses* (I should like just now to set aside the works of barbarous men who wrote in their romance languages) never happened nor can happen. Nevertheless these have passed as verisimilar through the use and authority of the writers. No less taken for the verisimilar are things which in the compositions are feigned *de novo*, brought into poetry by the usage of good poets and by the agreement of the world. This Aristotle indicated to us when he said that such was not far from the verisimilar; that many matters came into compositions which were beyond the verisimilar but, having been accepted by usage, can be commonly used without censure. He showed the same to us when he said that the wonderful was fitting to great heroic compositions and that falsehood serves them much more than truth.[56] He therefore taught us that the untrue ought to be feigned, since the wonderful originates from it.

The wonderful is derived with difficulty from the factual known as such by men; the wonderful is not to be found

Veri-similitude

in what occurs often and naturally, but is well derived from what appears to be impossible and, indeed, is taken for what happened, if not for the factual, at least for the fictional: such are the changing of men into trees, of ships into nymphs, of boughs into ships, of the joining of gods with human beings, and other like things which, although false and impossible, are nevertheless so accepted in usage that no composition is pleasurable in which such fables are not read.¶¶¶ Perhaps the poet is so called for this reason more than for any other. Indeed the name of poet is none other than that of maker. He is called poet not because of the verses but principally because of the matters that he made and feigned appropriate to poetry. If he should take only factual things and not feign *de novo*, he would lose the name of poet, since he would not create but only recite what was already made and what he could put before our eyes. The poet did not thus acquire the name, as Vida believed, according to the second of his *Ars Poetica*. Though it is also fitting for the poet to express the factual (as we shall say below), the name does not come from this but from the feigning and the making of fables and of men as they ought to be, as Aristotle teaches us in his *Poetics*. This shows that Aristotle has indeed seen with remarkable mastery what creates the excellence of the heroic poet.

The fables in the ancient Greek and Latin poets, especially the Greek, who with respect to the fictional have been most excellent, were often feigned by them *de novo*, according to what fit into their compositions, as in our time Pontanus has done. In all other requisites of a gifted and serious poet, Pontanus became great, so excellent is he in these particulars. Such is the quality of the fictional that often the fables and the untruths, though false and impossible, have more verisimilitude than the factual and possible, so that the latter seem to be the impossible.[57] But these fictions should be composed in such a way and joined together with such order that the feigned cannot be distinguished from the factual as regards the composition and the disposition, as Horace demonstrates in his *Ars Poetica*.[58] Aristotle said that the poet's aim was to induce good mores in the minds of men;[59] and he achieves this aim with his composition; whether of things false or of things true or of the true mingled with the false he makes use of what pertains to his art. Whereas the historian ought to write only the facts and actions as they are, the poet shows not things as they are but as they ought to be for the ameliorizing of life.*

This is the reason the poets, though they write of ancient things, nevertheless seek to fit them to the mores of their age, bringing in things unlike those of ancient times but fitting for theirs. For example, Vergil's Aeneas came from Troy where the forms of sacrificing, of celebrating funeral rites, and of arms were Asian rather than Italian; nevertheless the poet had the Trojans sacrifice, bury the dead, and fight according to the customs of Italy, not those before the founding of Rome but of the time of Octavian. Good poets have not only taken this license but have also given names to things of their time and have written these as if they belonged in that earlier time, as is seen in Homer and Vergil.

These customs have served the writers of Romances in some ways and this comes about because the poet writes (as I said) not of things that were or are, but of what ought to be, to please and delight at the same time, satisfying men of the age in which he writes, in a manner not permitted to those who write histories. Though Diodorus Siculus preferred history to poetry in the pleasing of mankind,⁶⁰ nonetheless I would trust Aristotle, who said that in pleasing poetry far surpassed history.⁶¹ Perhaps because history cannot be separated from the factual, one ought to write less of the vices than of the virtues, so that the reader may be more pleased than harmed. Where the poet with his creation imitates illustrious actions and puts forward not what is but what ought to be and these are suitably accompanied by the vicious, the horrible, and the miserable (this is no less valid for the heroic poet than for the tragic poet when the matter demands it), he purges our minds of a thousand passions and arouses us to virtue, as is seen in Aristotle's definition of tragedy.† ⁶²

Besides verisimilitude, therefore, that which is praiseworthy and honest in the whole work is to be considered, since otherwise the work would become loathsome and odious. In this respect all depends on the mores as to whether the actions are worthy of praise or of censure. For what we call thought or cogitation are the beginnings of human actions; and by custom men are said to be good or wicked, and by actions (as regards civil prosperity) are said to be happy or not; happy, those whose actions are full of virtue; unhappy, those entirely turned to crimes.‡

The Civil Function of the Poet — The function, then, of our poet, as regards the inducing of mores, is to praise virtuous actions and censure the vicious; and by means of the terrible and the miserable to make the vicious actions odious to him who reads.§ In these two respects the writers of Romances in our language are much ampler than the heroic Greeks and Latins, who only hinted at such censures and praises, whereas ours go further, especially in praising or censuring things of their time.

This custom (insofar as I can understand it) was first begun by Dante, who also surpassed the times before him. This was then accepted most graciously by our judicious Petrarch not only in his canzoni and sonnets, as in the canzone on Italy[63] and the sonnets on Rome,[¶64] but also in his *Triumphs*,[65] in which at many places he passes into digressions and then turns back skillfully to the subject he left. In this same manner our great and magnificent Ariosto has also succeeded, as he did admirably in putting into his work things beyond the scope of his primary purpose, but which contribute a marvelous beauty to his work. And such things will contribute much to the works of others who will put them in judiciously and decorously.

It is to be noted here that in these digressions, which contain jousts, tourneys, love affairs, beauties, passions of the mind, fields of battle, buildings, and other such things, the writer of the Romances is much more copious than either Vergil or Homer. In this respect he is more like Ovid (I speak of his *Metamorphoses*) than any other poet. It appears, then, that the character of this kind of composition searches for such beauty, so that the better poets of this language, introducing this custom, have given it authority and also, I shall not say boldness, but confidence to others to create the same, I believe that the first who did this in our language, in stanzas with greatness and dignity, was Politian, who, imitating Claudian with admirable grace, described the house of love.[66] After some years Egidio[67] succeeded him; in a beautiful metaphor of the chase, he described his love and the beauty of his lady in some stanzas which, if they had observed the niceties of the language as they have spirit and wit, not only would surpass those of Benivieni's on the chase,[68] as they do by far surpass them, but also would be unequaled.

Boiardo and Ariosto have practiced the same, so it can be said that such liberal abundance is fitting for this writing. In fact, grand ornamentation would detract from this kind of poetry if the writers of it did not put themselves through that rigor which Vergil passed through. In this the writer ought always to exercise prudence and to create so that in shunning the little he will not run into the excessive and thus yield to vice while seeking for that virtue which is the mean between too much and too little.

Although this attention is useful in every sort of description, it is most useful in occurrences of the doleful emotions and weeping. As these piteous emotions are created almost instantaneously, so in a moment they cease; to prolong them would not only be faulty but fruitless. It would be better to dry the tears under the eyes than to start them afresh. Furthermore, the poet ought not to extend himself in describing the establishing of military camps and the mobilizing of armies, since these are the historian's task, not the poet's, who takes these things for granted and who writes in his poem less of ordered troops than of battles, although it is fitting to make a catalog of arrayed peoples.** Nor is it necessary in describing buildings to try to delineate too minutely the art of architecture to the exclusion of what pertains to the poet. At this, above everything, he ought to aim, if he seeks praise, beyond those who bring in descriptions of mechanical things, with their cheapness, far from the usage and greatness of the heroic.†† There will be, then, Messer Giovambattista, for the writer of things serious and illustrious this firm rule: Leave out those descriptions which can produce irritation or are without pleasing quality or are unworthy of heroic grandeur and extend the poet beyond his limits.

The *Enargeia*[69] (to use the Greek term) of the poet among the Latins and us does not consist (as Trissino thought it did)[70] in writing minutely of every little insignificant thing whenever the poet writes heroically, but of things worthy of the greatness of the theme with which the poet is working. The virtue of *Enargeia* that we can call efficacious is achieved whenever neither words nor things are used unpleasantly. Although Homer (truly father of all poets as to matter and the ordering of it) lapsed many times in this respect, Vergil never did (although Catullus might have seen that in the *Epithalamium of Peleus and Thetis* he had thus minutely described the spinning of the Parcae). Vergil always attained to the grand and the magnificent and avoided the baseness unworthy of the heroic style; yet Trissino censures him for this reason, though he writes of Vergil not by name but under a veil. It was not remarkable that Trissino, intent on the low and base that is unfitting to a serious subject, would censure one who was not like him. Anyone who writes in our time ought therefore to consider that, as Vergil did not regard such things as suitable to his times and to the writer of serious subjects, so they are not suitable to us, for the reason we stated above when we discussed grandeur.‡‡

Enargeia

Decorum In these matters as in others, the poet ought always to have his eye on decorum, which is none other than what is fitting to places, times, and persons. Thus the ancient observers of nature said that decorum was that beauty, that grace, born from the forms of speaking when judgment and moderation were joined together and carried in themselves some manifestation of mores. These mores should be reflected in speech no less than the loveliness of color in a beautiful body; in other words, decorum is nothing other than grace and appropriateness. So the poet ought to be mindful not only of the actions but also of the speeches and responses which men carry on among themselves. For one would speak with a king in a different way than he would speak with a gentleman, and a king will answer another king as he would not answer one of his subjects or another lesser prince. He will speak to soldiers to urge them into battle otherwise than to quiet people who are in armed rebellion. In still a different way one captain will speak to another and one senator to another. So it happens with other kinds of persons, according to their blood, position, dignity, and authority, and according to places and times;§§ these things are left to the judgment of the writer, because estimation of this springs entirely from and rests in the writer's prudence. If such prudence does not guide him in writing, he will run into the ineptness exhibited by anyone who departed from that which he had learned from others and who, writing on his own, nevertheless showed everyone that the good came from a hand other than his own.

Decorum must be observed not only in the actions,

persons, places, times, as we have said, but also in language. Words are without force whenever nothing is under their blanket; nor can matter be made known without words. This principle should operate not only in the whole body of the work but in each part, as in the expositions, the invocations, the narrations, and in the other parts as they occur, so that each may have in itself what is particularly fitting to it. Therefore in things, in language, and in the whole and in the parts, he who seeks to gain praise as a writer must observe decorum carefully. Composition and arrangement of parts will be of little use if these parts are placed ineptly and if they sometimes lack decorum. Whenever the writer is not led by prudence in things and in words, he will lack decorum.

Because decorum, as we call grace combined with what is fitting, ought to be observed in the work according to its quality, the persons brought into it ought to be of the same quality as is the work. One should realize that in makeup the Romances are much more like Homer's *Odyssey* than the *Iliad*; in the Romances there is a greater variety in the quality of the persons than there would be if they were composed to resemble the *Iliad*. For that reason in the Romances are brought in frequent love affairs, and besides the kings and the queens and other great personages, nymphs, shepherds, shepherdesses, pages, boys, servants, hermits, peasants, and other kinds of folk. In the introduction of such persons one should consider well that the way they are introduced should be maintained to the end. Kings and queens should be majestic; persons of rank, of noble bearing and of dignified manners; nymphs, lovely and delighting in rivers, fields, and the things found there; shepherds, rude; shepherdesses, simple and uncultivated; boys, clever and cunning; children, timid; servants, pusillanimous, cowardly, and dishonest; soldiers, brave and menacing; captains, of much foresight and prudence; old men, prudent and wise in counsel; maidens, modest and timid; mothers, chaste and diligent; and so should be maintained from rank to rank the proper quality of the persons.[71]

It is true that unexpected events can occur, making the fierce humble, the lascivious continent, the timid bold, the bold timid; but there is need for close attention that decorum is not violated when such things happen. In Homer, Achilles by nature is rough, terrible, inexorable, but changes somewhat in nature when he gives Hector's body to Priam. In this the poet's prudence in perceiving the decorous changed that disposition of Achilles, making him return to what was native to him. Similarly Hercules is depicted by the Greeks as lascivious by nature; but he nonetheless returned Atlantis' daughters to him as virgins; and after the victory at Troy he gave Hesione to Telamon (the first to mount the enemy's wall) without requiring from her anything less than what was honest. Ulysses appeared worthy of censure by Aristotle,[72] when perceiving during the tempest that he was in danger of splitting the ship on Scylla or of being drowned in the sea, Ulysses grieved vehemently; nevertheless, I do not judge that the poet merits blame for representing him in such a way when in so grave a peril. Though Ulysses was strong and wise, he could reasonably fear and lament. These primary emotions of our spirits (let the Stoics say what they will), strong and wise though we are, are not in our power, especially when they proceed from a powerful and frightening occasion. It is therefore not out of decorum that Ulysses grieved in such grave circumstances. So much did this seem to Vergil, a writer of such high and mature judgment, to fit decorum and verisimilitude that he too depicted Aeneas, in the first book of the *Aeneid*, as doing likewise; he showed him also in the second book as moved to wrath and wishing to kill Helen as the one responsible for the downfall of Troy. Francesco Campano wrote excellently of this matter against the opinion of the commentators on Vergil, and (in my judgment) very reasonably.[73]

But, to return to Aristotle, I have wondered many times why he censures Homer for depicting Ulysses as lamenting death in the sea, since he said in the third of his *Ethics* that just as an honorable death ought not to cause fear in the strong,[74] so a situation in which there is no place for valor or fortitude can only be grievous for him. If one laments the ending of his life in such a manner, he does nothing less than would a strong man; among those kinds of death in which the strong man is to grieve, Aristotle includes death in a storm at sea. So manifest a contradiction as this in an author of such prudence has made me think that Aristotle did not intend in it to censure Homer, since, so far as I see, Aristotle in this place in the *Poetics* is not speaking of the epic but of tragedy, as the examples given of Menalippe[75] and of Orestes show. Since he gives here an example of the aspect of conduct that is not fitting, I think he is giving us an example from tragedy, not from epic, and perhaps intends to mention the little prudence and attention of any poet who would depict shipwrecked Ulysses in the scene not lamenting as a strong man would in such circumstances, but uttering excessive cries and laments unworthy of the manly mind. It could well be that such a poet was like those of whom Atheneus speaks in XIV.[76] Nevertheless I leave to better judges the verdict about what in this matter appears better to them. I shall not, however, refrain from saying that Lucan (who was partly imitated by Trissino in the tempest of Giustino in the third of his *Italia*), perhaps fearful of this censure and believing that Homer had been reprimanded in it, depicted Caesar, in the fifth of his *Pharsalia*, as courageous in a storm in which he had entered voluntarily, though the prudent pilot had forecast it for him by many signs. Caesar would undoubtedly have been blameworthy if he had lamented on what he had done voluntarily; but whether to enter into the obvious danger of the storm, where there was no place for valor or fortitude, was a bold deed meriting more mature consideration than it is pertinent to discuss at this point. It is true that in Caesar's impetuosity Lucan observed decorum much better than Trissino did in the episode of Giustino, who, though going into the storm willingly, is then made to lament in the way that we see. Surely it was an example of irregular habit, since Trissino does not show him to be of this kind when he was put in voluntary danger.

Now to return to a discussion of that aspect of decorum concerning matter (of language we shall speak more later): One should realize that in works of this nature, as in all the Greek and Latin heroic poems, difficulties are encountered which need more than human action to be solved. This part of decorum Vergil, Homer, and other good authors who wrote of heroic matters of one action and also of many (as did Ovid in *Metamorphoses*, if he can be counted among these authors) have handled well, because they introduced their gods, who have impeded some improprieties and provoked others, have created disorder, quieted discords, incited battles, hindered treaties, kindled furious acts and unexpected displays of violence. The poet who writes Romances of Christian matters, on the other hand, is not allowed to do so. The majority of our God and his ministering angels does not permit us to invoke them and interpose them in our angers and wars, having them favor one and condemn another to death, as did a poet of our time who brought in the Virgin Mother kneeling before her Son and praying that he would consent to the death of many thousands of Christian people. Another introduced Christ as prophesying that his life and death and all his miraculous works would be written about by a poet who would be born on the author's own native river.[77] This is far from all decorum and piety and is unfitting to the Christian religion in which we were born and in which we grew up. Though it may be granted that we read at times, both in the ancient law and in Christian histories, that God has done such things through the divine will, this was in matters that were worthy of the hand of God, either in his mercy or in his divine justice, not for fables feigned by a poet. I cannot see that it is permissible to mix, among our feigned and fabled matter, persons of such majesty and reverence, whom we should never name except with the highest respect. Seeing this, writers who in Romances dealt with Christian subjects feigned by them (so as not to fall into this unseemliness) have introduced the fates; and instead of the false and lying ancient gods (as Dante said) have brought in infernal spirits and feigned their incantations. By means of these they have secured in their works the same effects that the Greek and Latin poets made earlier with the power of their gods. To give such power to a demon or to one who professes the black arts seems to me to border on the omnipotent and to be appropriate only to God. I should say (deferring always to better judgment) that the writers of Romances have brought in these enchantments and sorceries much more reasonably than if they had tried to bring in celestial angels

—substances by their nature most pure and without the mortal passions that occur in us because of the variety in our complexions.

It seems to me, further, that it would not be right to give pagan names to the angels, calling them Pallases, Junos, Venuses, Marses, Irises; besides that, in divine matters it would mix paganism with Christianity. This is to be avoided by those of our religion so that they may not set a bad example contrary to decorum. This practice also would make these celestial spirits subject to the vanities and deceiving fictions of the pagan gods and would turn Christian things (full of true religion) into jests and fables.

If the poet who deals with romantic materials chooses ancient matter upon which to build his poem—matter which is in the categories of these religions or ancient superstitions—he can without censure (it seems to me) include in it Venus, Juno, Jove, Pallas, and all the other deities esteemed and reverenced in that time among people who let themselves be deceived by such fabricated falsehoods and who remained as if blind in those shadows.

Rhetorical Schemes I could at this point take up the images and turns (*ruote*) which some have devoted themselves to propounding to us, since from them could be drawn the materials of composition, and the figures of speech and the ideas (seeking to show with obscure modes what is easily shown by good writers) which have made thorny and rough the road to art that Aristotle, Horace, and other esteemed authors have made level and smooth, especially Aristotle in the *Poetics* and the *Rhetoric*. But I do not wish (traveling their road with these obstacles) to retard the course of fine genius, except to say I have clearly seen that such as these, promising much and understanding little, have always been under dreams and fancies and, speaking wholly in the abstract and enigmatically, have with their evasions confused some of good genius. With these fabricated appearances some have been deceived; in the shadows they have never known clarity. In the hope of such promises but never seeing any tangible results, they spend their time fruitlessly, not otherwise than those who to learn grammar have wasted themselves in Scotus'; or like those who to grasp the disciplines have been exposed to the art of Raymond Lully, who in the name of teaching them discipline to which they have devoted themselves, so leads them into the shadows that, if they are occupied with these incredibly bad tales, they never know the light of knowledge and are like moles.

Our forefathers gave us the laws of letters by which everything can be easily analyzed and reduced to a beautiful design, and we have the principles by which we can shape all we wish to write; thus we can pass along to others the way to draw the subject-matter without these monstrous images and useless evasions. Instead of such imaginations, I would rather propose those writers who, without so many turns and images, have not shown us the artifice about which those make so much ado, nor have merely promised us but have given us the true form of speaking. To those who would have asked for such precepts, I believe these writers would have said to us that what pertained to good composition would be found in their works. And indeed they would have replied most aptly, since such fantasies have not proved useful to writers except for a certain vainglory of wishing to show that one knows more than others about a matter of no consequence, and for being able to deceive others into thinking the useful is derived from them and to prate swellingly about the marvelous compositions of excellent writers. The good writers, beyond the knowledge of these things and using judgment as a guide, and nature accompanied by admirable art and by exercise of it, not with these gyrations, made their works such as we now have them.

A beautiful and useful labor was the work of our most eloquent Bartholomeo Riccio,[78] who was the first to give writers excellent laws concerning materials and words and showed the artistic form to be observed; beautiful also was that of Nizzolio[79] in his analyses and observations on the works of Cicero; beautiful was that of Erittreo on the divine poem of the Mantuan Homer; and beautiful above all others in that [Latin] language was Robert Estiennes's *Thesaurus*. And beautiful in the Italian was our most diligent Alunno's observations on Petrarch and Boccaccio[80] and his *La Fabbrica del Mondo*. All these authors and those like them have put into their observations and analyses not wheels and figures but the forms of speech of the better writers, leaving to the judgment of anyone who aims to write well the skill of using them and of following the example of the better writers.

I should like, therefore, for gentle spirits to exercise themselves in such things as are observed in good authors, together with the precepts, so that by noting and obeying their virtues they may learn the true form of speech. These writers will draw from them what is useful much more than from such images and figures, which would suffice to occupy a man's whole lifetime and even then would not inspire them to make one verse worthy of the name. Good writing is not an involved mystery; nature has planted the seeds of it in our minds and these spring up of themselves not indeed in composition, which is done with great diligence, but in acts of reasoning, which arise every day not only in men of noble birth but in men of humbler origin. If we will cultivate such seeds with art, by reading the works of good authors and by practicing to become like them, they will produce those fruits that would never be produced if writers are occupied with those things—I do not know whether I should call them extreme teachings or vain superstitions—which are worshiped as oracular by those easily dominated by such foolish masters.

From the good authors are had in part the materials and in part the way of finding the new; also the way to handle them artistically and to set them felicitously on paper. From the good authors are derived what went before, what follows after, and what is added; from them also is derived the way to join the parts of the work, to give to the words a pleasing position, and whatever else is useful and necessary for good writing. He who sets before himself the good writers, Messer Giovambattista, has no need of such schemes of artifices in whose wheels, as in a mill, writers are caught and, as they are continually whirled about, lose the light of the intellect. May they avoid these labyrinths in which those who have entered have acted like unhappy wits captivated by the notions of Hermogenes. These, when they discuss such minutiae, seem like new Demostheneses, but when they try hard to compose an oration, they make the most inane things in the world, like anything except an oration. I do not say this because I censure those precepts necessary for good writing. Aristotle, Cicero, and other ancients gave us those that pertain to useful and profitable instruction. And these precepts some other contemporaries have given and still give, who, leaving ostentation, seek to help, like teachers of one who does not know, and do not wish to show themselves more learned than anyone else (useless to one who seeks to learn). Nor do I censure the forms that Aristotle in the *Poetics* called Ideas, since these ought to be considered carefully by the poet. But the mode that is fitting, useful, proper is not exhibited by these involved gyrations.

One who wishes to learn can do no more with this minute and useless diligence than did Alexander the Great with the vain dexterity of one who, in order to throw a chick-pea, set it on the point of a needle; or than did the good judges of the four-horse chariots of Calicratidas or of Myrmecides, which were entirely covered by the wings of a fly. For this is simply a useless waste of time. Moreover, the poet has no need of such minute considerations. Aristotle indicated this to us when he said that the poet could use these forms without doctrine and without art, but that the orator could not use them without much art and the greatest study. It seemed to Aristotle that such things in the poet should be more of prudence than of art, and that nature could do more than excessive diligence. This is as we usually say, that nature produces the poets, but art makes the orators. I say that good authors, such as the two better Tuscans[81] (to speak now only of this language) and others after them, such as Bembo and Ariosto, through their natural inclination for poetry without this art, with the guidance of their nature (without which no one should ever undertake to write), thereafter acquired judgment; and through learned disciplines, the reading of good authors, and sustained exercise wrote most excellently and will mold others who will follow in their footsteps and will not grow old as on the rocks of the Sirens in the intricacies of that "art," by which no one has yet written anything worth reading. Nor do I believe that anyone may do so by means of these inanities, since anyone who has any genius will not wish to be shackled with such fabricated intricacies nor to be deceived by such make-believe as he who reasons little has given the name of art. Those who with ease propose to teach us these things cause us to grow old in the ignorance in which inability to be free of such fabricated confusions holds us. Hence any man who would become a learned and artistic writer by these vanities remains a child. As Plato said to Anniceris of Cyrene, one who is intent on minute things necessarily overlooks important things.[82]

They become only frenetic who by the example of these authors make so many fantasies on the works of Petrarch and of other writers that, for every sonnet on which they choose to comment, they compose a whole volume. In the name of philosophers they would draw out not only the Platonic and Peripatetic philosophies and all that is contained within the golden circle of all the disciplines—called by the better wits the study of humanity—but also the cabalistic superstitions and all that is in divine and human laws, making chimeras and fantasies completely foreign to the meaning of the things on which they comment. Not to speak of others, there were and are today some who, departing from the true sense, make such fabrications on some of Petrarch's things that these appear spiritual; and call them marvels; and find therein the voice of love, or nature, or Jove, or Juno, or desire, or beauty, or the sun, or the sky; and such other things they would derive which have never been written from the beginning of the world up to their age. Petrarch would no more have subscribed to these visionary things if he had seen them than he would

Absurdity of Excessive Allegoresis

to one who made him an ecclesiastic, vesting him as a minor friar, girding him with a cord, and putting wooden clogs on his feet. This is bad usage indeed and unworthy of acceptance by intelligent men! Although such exhibitions may show a man to be learned and versed in various disciplines, they show him to be without judgment in applying them without moderation. I do not know, Messer Giovambattista, what such men think they are doing. As for me, I think there is no writing in the world so inane about which such fabricated dreams cannot be made, whenever a learned and ingenious man wishes to waste his time on them.

You and I knew Mariano Buonincontro of Palermo, a man of incisive and lively intelligence, who at an early age was a recipient here in Ferrara of an honorary doctor of laws. To make fun of such geniuses, this man made (as you know) the most beautiful sonnets in the world, as to diction and rhythm, but which said nothing and were without sense. Then he allowed them to be issued under the name of some fine man; he himself moved among the others and let it be known that he wished to discuss them, saying that their sense was marvelous. He therefore induced everyone to make fantastic judgments about them. Among the others he issued one that seemed to be on the death of the illustrious Signora the Duchess of Urbino. Here it is.

> I piu lievi, che Tigre, pensier miei
> Scorgendo il cor, che tra doi petti intiero
> Tiene un pensier, poi che gl'ingombra il vero
> Et folle error, fuggono i casi rei.
> Et benche da gli antichi Semidei
> Biasmato fosse ovunque ogn'altro è fiero
> Monte d'orgogli. Ahi lassa, io gia non spero

> Gioir in quel disir, c'haver vorrei.
> Onde dal crudo suon stancata l'alma
> Germoglia in me l'ardir, poi che s'agghiaccia,
> Et scalda hor quinci, hor quindi il caldo gelo.
> Et io del verde fior perdo la traccia;
> Me l'asconde lo sdegno in picciol velo
> Tolta da i tronchi error la grave salma.
>   Benche, chi tien la palma
> De gli inganni morta', brami con forza
> Condur a l'empio fin l'amara scorza.[83]

He said that this was a work of rare genius. Spreading abroad about it some things to make it seem to be his, he induced a very learned but injudicious Sienese to make on it a commentary divided into four books, which is still read. So point by point, which made no sense and said nothing, that fellow spun out stuff such as he had never read in all his life.

I shall not be irksome if I add to this sonnet, which (as I have said) is in the hands of men with such excellent commentary, this other one which gave and still gives one whom you know so much to do. Although he was told it was a fraud, he was unwilling to admit that he had been so foolish as to think there was a marvelous meaning in it and thus persisted in his ravings about it. He would have everyone think that it says much when it was made to say nothing; he entered into a wilderness of Apollo's laurel and Venus' myrtle and into the forge of Vulcan with the most beautiful fantasies ever to come to a dreaming man's mind. Here is the sonnet.

> Da chi fe indivinar gia le Sibille
> Venne il sospetto, la temenza, c'hora
> Afflige il core a chi v'inchina e adora,
> Per poter un di haver hore tranquille.

> Et se gli manda faci a mille a mille
> La crudelità, che vuol, ch'amando mora
> Chi vive in foco, & è di vita fuora;
> Che gli giova pregar, che non si stille?
> Ai giustitia divina, come puoi
> Non far quel, che far dei? qual fiero spirto
> Fu quel, che indusse questa peste al mondo?
> Deh fuss'io stato all'hor posto nel fondo
> Dell'Acheronte, che fui qiunto al Mirto,
> Ch'ombra mortal mi fa co rami suoi.[84]

Some make particular compositions which include grand and obscure conceits needing long and careful exposition; for example, Lucretius' Latin poem and Benivieni's canzone in the vulgar which he composed on the subject that the greater Pico gave him and that Pico himself later commented on, to open up the road to Platonic philosophy, which he and Ficino, in the time of Lorenzo de' Medici (patron of disciplines and studies in humane letters), drew out of the shadows in which it had been for many years. However, Pico himself was contrary in many respects to the thought of Ficino, as would be clear if his commentary on this canzone is read as he wrote it;[85] and it, after Pico's death, common friends of Pico and Ficino had not suppressed the divergencies, as may be seen by those who have read the commentary as Pico wrote it in his own hand. Such was likewise Dante's intention when he commented on the canzoni of his *Banquet*; there was no need to become frenzied in commenting on them, since the aim in writing them was clear. Perhaps for this same purpose Tolomei[86] composed the stanzas on the degrees of love which Plato showed us. In these, Tolomei testified very clearly how much he would alter if he should undertake the writing of such things in trying to unfold the merit of Plato's genius and the riches of his mind.

Expositions so intended ought not to be censured; but expositions ought to be brief, since lengthy ones are an annoyance in this language as they were in Latin (if the subject did not merit, as, for example, Macrobius' commentary of Cicero's *Dream of Scipio* and Hierocles' on the verses of Pythagoras).[87] In this respect the Greeks were too verbose, especially those who commented on Homer. Some of these run into exceedingly long commentaries; others go into such fantastic matters that (like other Chrysippuses)[88] they would allegorize every story in Homer, reading meanings into the poem which he perhaps never imagined. Landino would do the same for Vergil,[89] but little success followed him, not because he did not show himself learned and intelligent but because the Italians have similar discourses in abundance, and it is not our intention to linger over these. They may leave this pretension to the Greeks, who in order to make their fable-writers and poets appear more than human are taken with these vanities. These people do not deserve more praise from good judges than did Chrysippus, who tended to see miracles in every story he encountered; accordingly he was duly restrained by the better philosophers. Perhaps I also shall not be without critics for having in this part gone further than pertains to the primary subject; but the reason is that these two overdiligent efforts came from the same source, my desire to help. Therefore it behoves me to return to the images of which I spoke before.

The young ought to be warned diligently about such appearances of ease and not to give ear to such fabrications, whose authors have not composed more than what is moderately pleasurable, perhaps less so, lapsing often into great carelessness concerning matters of language. But with study and exercise (without exercise genius rusts), they should seek to make their writing so excellent that they may become a rule to themselves; indeed to compose continually and to consider unceasingly what has been put together makes one use his materials as did the ancients—by an established rule.

It would be fitting at this point to speak of the recognition [*anagnorisis*] of the terrible, of the pitiable, of the change from a happy to an unhappy state and vice versa, and of the marvelous, without which this kind of poem [the Romance] is no less excellent than tragedy. But since in our treatment of the qualities of tragedy we have (if I am not in error) amply expounded that matter, showing what pertains to the heroic and what to tragedy, we shall proceed now without saying anything further on the subject. Now that we have put together the bones of the body of the Romances, filled up the hollows, and smoothed down the fatness, as far as the form of such compositions is concerned, the time is at hand to be concerned with the beauty of the delicate skin's colors.

Elocution It remains therefore to speak of elocution and of the manner of expressing with fitting words the thoughts that the poet will have apprehended and ordered in his mind. This matter is wholly in the judgment, in the choice of the words, in the joining of these, in the figures of speech, in the sound, in the numbers, and in the other qualities that either pertain to the words or are to be considered about them.

Since elocution has the same place in composition as the skin does in the human body, the poet ought to put his effort on this part, under which stand all the others, as nature does on the skin of the body. Just as nature, a judicious creatress (by virtue of the intelligence which rules her) of that which she produces, took great care to make this skin soft, pliable, and delicate, and to give it the grace of proper colors so that it appears pleasing to our eyes and makes delightful all that is under it, so the poet should put much talent and study on everything pertaining to words. Since they clothe our ideas and carry them from the intellect to the eyes, they ought to be adorned with all the beauty that the industry of the writer can give them. Although in this, no less than in other particulars, one ought to shun such superfluous diligence, lest what one would make good becomes bad, and lest excessive desire to embellish results in fastidiousness. Negligence neatly practiced is sometimes better than too much diligence.

We behold with pleasure, Messer Giovambattista, the sight of a beautiful woman, of living color, pure, clean, without spot. We are no less pleased if this vision is attended by modesty and gentility from the art of the lady, an adornment that she so adds to her native beauty that it seems not made artificially but born with her. But if there is so much adorning (as we see today in many) that natural grace is smothered and only art is seen, the result is an odious lady who, seeking to please, so displeases that a sane eye would rather admire a simple shepherdess with no ornament than the overadorned lady. The same also applies to words, with respect to their ornaments, since they are more pleasing and delightful to the degree that they are close to nature and have in them the least artifice. To state a general rule about this: The most beautiful artifice is to conceal it with such art that it can scarcely be seen.

Now that we have drawn this generality about the

beauty of words as simple and used alone, I shall come to particular matters about how they are joined together. First, one should know that words were discovered so that (as Horace said) they may be interpreters of our minds and carry, by the hearing of the ears, our thoughts and ideas to others' minds. This is why Aristotle said that words are none other than the signs of the passions which we have in the mind, calling as passions what we now call ideas or thoughts or concepts. In his *Poetics* he called passion *sentenza* (thought),[90] as I showed where I spoke of dramatic matters.[91] As words serve us to represent our concepts, so letters (written characters) serve the concept and the words to reveal our thoughts not only to those present but to those distant and also to those who will come after us for many centuries. We exercise much care and diligence when we speak with those in our company, because our conversation may please and delight them; we ought to exercise even greater care when we write. For the word, as soon as it is uttered, vanishes, staying under judgment only as it is heard; and being aided by the spirit, by grace, and by the speaker's action, does not often allow its defects to be seen. Writing, however, always remains under the eyes and under the reader's judgment, without the aids that the spoken word has when it is uttered. It therefore has no external quality that can give it distinction if it does not carry it in itself. This is why our poet ought to be diligent in finding words that have in themselves such grace, splendor, and embellishment as to be able to delight and make pleasing the subject that they carry along with them to the minds of readers of good taste. He who is not so diligent should refrain from writing, since, if his compositions are lacking in this diligence, he will see that they are dead before they are even born. The author who sets out his thoughts on paper without splendor of words will see the funeral and burial of his fame, which he believed would be immortal for such composition.

In this respect, therefore, the first concern of the writer ought to be centered on what Caesar said was the first principle of good writing, namely, the choice of words, which involves not only entire words but also the elements and the syllables that compose them, since these are the roots of beautiful and artistic elocution. Just as there is no tree without roots, so there is no artistic writing without considering these things. But I shall not belabor this matter, which has been treated with much grace and diligence by our Italians, among whom Monsignor Bembo with remarkable skill has given it great attention. Our language owes no less to him than to its fathers, Dante, Petrarch, and Boccaccio. If they generated it, he, as we have already said in our *Epigrams*, revived it, rescued it from death, and gave it as much light and authority as almost all the other writers before him. In his *Prose* he has spoken of the art of writing and of the rules governing the language.[92] He has shown abundantly everything concerning words and letters (characters); and in his poems he has shown the art of placing them in literary works. For this part (of my discourse) I have reread his *Prose* for his precepts and reread his poems to see how these precepts ought to be used.

Therefore, relying on the reading of this judicious writer for knowledge of the qualities of words, I shall say nothing further, except that even if it seems more laborious than need be to measure and analyze so minutely characters,

Choice of Words

syllables, and words, it is nevertheless so necessary that anyone who does not give his attention to such cannot write artistically. But usage, the master of all things, and nature aided by it, make this tediousness pleasant. Our ears, or rather our minds, by means of the sounds sent through hearing, have naturally in themselves a certain measure of the sounds of words which generates the judgment. If the judgment is aided by usage and by diligence, it becomes perfected. As soon as the mind, than which nothing is faster, has composed the sentence, it sees and recognizes the words with which the sentence is expressed. And this usage is taught both by reading excellent authors and by composing assiduously. Leaving out either the one or the other makes the wit not only sluggish and crude but sterile of everything and without taste.

We ought, therefore, with composing and with assiduous reading of good authors, so to train the ears to words that we shall know how to make the best judgment of them and to discern with what order and what measure they should be joined together, so that the verse will be rhythmical with proper sound and have that harmony which depends on both sound and metrical rhythm, as in the proper place we shall demonstrate more fully.

As we have said above, the observations of Francesco Alunno aid wonderfully in the choice of words; in his *Ricchezze,* his *Fabbrica,* and his *Osservationi* on Petrarch,[93] he alleviates with his industry the labor for students of language in such a way that I believe anyone who aims at writing will feel infinitely obliged to him. However much the choice of words results from assiduous reading of good authors, no one is so versed in reading them that in composing he does not often need to be informed about not only simple words but also how they are joined, how their position is determined, and what is their use in verse and in prose. This diligent man did this more assiduously and pleasingly than any other writer who undertook such a task in any other language.

Since we are speaking of the verses suitable to the Romances and not of the others—setting aside other qualities of verses—we should inquire into the kind appropriate for such a poem. It seems to me that verses of eleven syllables are those with which such subjects should be treated, since this is the best, the most perfect measure, of our language for writing heroic works such as we are speaking of here. Those of seven syllables are not suited to serious subjects and those of twelve syllables, because of their redundant-syllable [*sdruccioloso*] ending, lack gravity and debase the work in which they appear; but drawn from a few certain words, which Petrarch used, and accompanied by those which do not have a *sdruccioloso* ending, these verses create in some places in his *Canzoniere* and *Triumphs* a soft, smooth sound.

Suitable Verse

The writer of Romances therefore should confine himself to verses of eleven syllables, for these are most fitting for serious and heroic thoughts, and should shy away from the *sdrucciolosi* and those usually called mute, which are of ten syllables. If one of these two must be used, as is sometimes the case when the place and the situation we are talking about asks for it, I am more satisfied with the verse having a mute syllable than with the *sdruccioloso*.

Avoidance of Sdruccioli

The former carries with it a weighty and serious effect; the latter, a low and languid effect that is little fitting to such a work, except to the extent that the poet, to his liking, should wish to include one of them to show that he knows it and how to use it. This he ought to do rarely. It is perhaps better to refrain altogether from its use and confine himself to verses of eleven syllables. But since these can be either with or without rhyme—and those with rhyme are of various qualities—one must see which is the one suitable to these compositions.

Unrhymed Verse   To begin with those without rhyme: I think they are in no way fitting to heroic matter, since, it seems to me, the best manner of verses in our language is appropriate for works of such importance, so that here may be seen the art, the study, and the thought (without running to fault) of the composer; besides, this carries in itself the sweetness of sound and gravity with measure and with the other qualities that belong to the sublime. These qualities neither are nor can be in the kind of verses that Trissino, the inventor of them, called *sciolti* (unbound) because freed from rhymes.[94] This is true because rhyme is the sweetness and harmonious softness that our verses can have. If it is removed the verse remains so much like free discourse that it does not appear to be verse, so much is it without beauty, sweetness, and heroic dignity. This does not belong to a poem that seeks much grace and sweetness with much dignity. These qualities cannot be found in verse that is more fitting for everyday speech than for a composition that strives for thoughtfulness and judiciously artistic grandeur. The inventor of such verses admitted that they were most fitting for the dramatic, since they were shown to be free and loosed from all thought and appear as born for common speech. If this is true, how can anyone think that such kind of verse can be fitting for a poem which would be full of grandeur, beauty, and dignity?

It seems to me that Monsignor Bembo, as judicious a writer as any in our language, spoke the truth when he said to me at Bologna that, just as Trissino should be thanked for having given such verses to the theatre, so he deserved no thanks for having made the people of our tongue so careless as to use them in works other than dramatic; that conquered by slothfulness in avoiding the designing of fitting rhymes, they had chosen such verses for the heroic. In my opinion, bad judgment is shown by those who transfer these verses from the theatre to grand subjects which, if they lack rhymes, lack everything that makes the whole work pleasurable. Those who deal with grand and noble themes with verses formed in such a way show that they love license more than the regulated linking and the order of rhymes. This can be only censurable. It is very difficult (whoever tries it can bear witness) to give to a grand theme of some length rhymes that are not empty and ineffective but significant and fitting, or taken from outside in such a way that they accompany the sense with proper harmony and so correspond throughout the whole work. It appears that to avoid effort (I believe this to be indubitable) such writers are addicted to meters that fall unthinkingly from the mouth of whoever talks and from the pens of whoever writes with no intention of making verse. So I have pointed out—a long time ago—that in the speech and the writing not only of noble and learned persons but of the stupid and base who speak and write, there is no one who writes familiar letters, no matter how base and ignorant, who does not fall inadvertently into such free verse, so familiar is this kind of verse in everyday speech and writing; but how removed from the harmoniously rhythmical verse appropriate to the heroic! Some have thought that such verses are not verses at all, but they are; and to the extent that they are suitable for the theatre, they are not suitable for the heroic.

Now that we are discussing *sciolti*, it seems to me that those are injudicious who have introduced into drama the free verses called *sdruccioli*. If the free verses are suitable to the drama because of frequent occurrence in everyday speech, the *sdrucciolo* ought to be totally unfitting, as a rhythm that has no point of resemblance to the everyday conversation of men, because one will speak or write a whole day without one *sdrucciolo* verse falling from his mouth or pen, whereas hundreds of those of eleven syllables will occur. In considering the origin of this error of introducing *sdruccioli* in drama, I have succeeded in finding no explanation except that while these dramatic poets paid attention to the number of syllables and to the ending of the Greek and Latin iambic verse, they took care only that their verse was similar in both things to the iambic and were content that these verses were of twelve syllables, for those of twelve are true iambics; and that they have the ending of the *sdrucciolo*, which comes from the short syllable before the long. They did not consider, then, whether or not our common speech admits these numbers, as the Latin iambics do.

But to return to the place we left off: This kind of verse should be avoided as unsuited to the kind of poem we are discussing. Granted that these people say that seeking to arrange rhymes in works often results in low and base verses, unsuitable for the heroic; nevertheless, I say quite the contrary, that rhymes make verse magnificent when written by one who has the manner and the mastery of using them well. Whoever does not understand this or cannot do it because he does not have the natural talent for it, ought rather to cease composing than to labor at a form of verse not suitable to the subject, because to use high-sounding, clamorous, bombastic, high-spirited words, as do many (not only in heroic matters but even in country matters) to aggrandize their verses is not to give something suitable to lofty subject-matter, although it appears so to such poets. The sweetness of the metrical rhythm and of the sound of the rhymes accompanied by gravity and fittingness of words is much more excellent and appropriate than the other. The desire to avoid hard work or their lack of knowledge that they are not capable of writing poems has caused them to yield to this practice, although to him who looks rightly at it, it appears without the grandeur of heroic rhythm. That this practice is the cause is shown clearly by the stanzas on heroic matters which any of these writers have made who have sometimes written in *versi sciolti* the ideas that belong to the stanzas. Because of this, conquered by labor and abandoned by nature, they have written ninety rhymes out of a hundred which have nothing to do with the subject of the stanza, but fall at the end only to make the sound and the rhyme; therefore it happens (we shall say more about this below) that half of the verse is useless, at times two or three verses in one stanza. I could adduce so many examples of these things that you could perhaps not ask me for more, but I restrain myself because I do not wish anyone on account of my judgment to be displeasing to himself or to be blamed by others for my judgment or displeasure. I shall leave consideration of this to you, Messer Giovambattista, and to those who know how to discern virtue from vice, and the excellent from the blameworthy.

Leaving, then, these *versi sciolti*, let us inquire which verses with rhyme are fitting for this composition. Since we do not need to consider here sonnets or canzoni or madrigals or ballades or other kinds of poems that are written not to deal with a subject at length (as the Romance does) but because they stand instead of the Latin lyrics, we can turn only to the kind of verses suited to continuous matter.

Terza Rima and Ottava Rima These, it seems to me, can be of two sorts (until someone appears to show us a better form): one, called terzetto or catena; the other, called ottava rima or stanza. If at this point I had the power to choose between these two kinds of verse, I would adhere to the terzetto, since this kind of verse seems to me, when in rhyme that is well used and where it is fitting, to be graver and grander than anything else in our language up to now in its possibility for dealing with a long and heroic subject. This appears in the example of Dante, who was perhaps its inventor, and in Petrarch, who borrowed it from Dante and made it lighter and softer as he thus made everything he took from the ancients. Yet Dante expounded (though roughly enough) philosophy and theology in a poetic manner in this kind of verse. In the same kind Petrarch wove with remarkable thread his ever-praised *Triumphs*. But because the writers of Romances have left the catena and practiced the stanza, which is judged by many to be like the lyric verses—a discovery (as some would have it) by the Sicilians or (as others say) by the Provençals; and in order not to depart from the usage of good authors who have written in it and have given authority to this kind of rhyme with their works (the first of whom was perhaps Boccaccio, who in like verse composed, infelicitously enough, his *Theseid* and other works); even I shall accept the ottava rima as that established by authority of the poets and by usage (from which it would be presumptuous to depart) and as that which alone appears fitting for this sort of poetry.

Though there are those who say that this kind of rhyme is unsuitable for the heroic, since it is customary to sing the stanza to the accompaniment of the lyre, their reasoning is not enough to make me change my opinion, since the heroic verses of Homer were also sung to the lyre, as we said above, and nonetheless do not fail for that reason to be heroic verses. I cannot see that any kind of verses in any language cannot be sung accompanied by the lyre; and yet they remain of their own nature and do not become lyrics. This should occur even less in our language in that all of our complete verses (I speak of those of the better poets) are only of eleven syllables and do not have the variety of feet found in Greek and Latin. Omitting consideration of the other types of rhyme, we shall now discuss only this type accepted by usage.

Ottava Rime Suited to Romances

First I say that, searching my mind for the reason why these compositions are more suited to the ottava rima than to the catena, to which, we have said, Dante and Petrarch gave such authority and reputation in their writings on serious matters, it seems to me (letting, however, everyone judge according to his own view) that this has happened because the first composers of Romances devoted themselves to singing (or at least feigning to sing) their compositions before their princes. Thus there was need of rest and stillness for the speaker and his hearers. This peace and quiet could not inhere so tidily or so fully in the catena until it ended, since the little rest between one terzetto and another and which ought to exist in the stanza between two verses and two verses is momentary and not suitable for the taking of as much breath as both hearer and speaker need. Therefore the writers or reciters of Romances chose the stanza, which embraces a seemly part of the subject in its eight verses and with its pleasingly harmonious ending gives both the speaker and the hearer place and time to take a breath, without interrupting the order and continuity of the work. This occurs because after the ear is accustomed to such a pause and to the agreement of the last two rhymes, which offer wonderful delight, the ear awaits them with admirable and supreme desire from stanza to stanza, not otherwise than the ear accustomed to the meter of Vergil anticipates, now dactyls, then spondees under which according to the course of the matter the mind of the reader or hearer is able to get both a pleasing rest and a fitting continuity to that which remains to be said.

This may also be perceived more clearly in the elegies, which go forward two by two throughout and so give continuity with rest and are in this respect like the stanza. So powerful is this in the stanza with respect to readers and hearers that he who would compose such subjects in verses without this ottava rima would beyond doubt be little praised and little pleasing to those hearing and reading his compositions. Deciding, then, for these reasons, that such poems must be written in ottava rima, it remains for us to see what is to be considered in arranging his ideas in this sort of verse in such a way that will equally profit and delight.

Granted that it is necessary at this point to discuss the harmony and pleasingness of the words and the placement of the accents, which give metrical rhythm to verse, I refer to what Monsignor Bembo has written about it, and others following him, and I also in a book where I discussed the qualities of numbers in various kinds of composition.

At present I shall abandon this discussion and shall begin other matters worth considering for speech. Of these I believe the first and most important is the discovering of the words and the rhymes by which thoughts are set forth. These ought to be joined to please and delight with profit those who read and hear. As the profit is derived from the thoughts and the matters dealt with in the narrative, so the words, besides the expression of the thought, are entirely for pleasurable beauty, and among them most especially the rhymes. And this method will aid the writer marvelously if we assume that he wishes to close some part of his narrative at the end of a stanza; he will consider carefully what words the subject of the stanza he wishes to compose carries with it. Having considered it, he ought with great care to see that from the words he chooses to set forth the subject on paper he can get appropriate and natural rhymes; and if he can get them, as he often can, he should compose the stanza with them, because with them it will come out only pleasing and refined. Since a matter often carries in itself two or three words able to create harmonies of sound, the composer ought to use those which can be mated most fittingly with their companions whether his own or taken from outside, as we shall discuss further below.

Rhymes

The good poet ought not to be content with having harmony of rhymes by whatever means is offered to him; he ought also to have it so that these rhymes seem to have been produced by nature itself to express the thought. He ought to exercise the utmost diligence that the rhymes, together with the rest of the words, will so exhibit the subject that it appears the matter was set out in prose with these words. There should be no straining for the rhymes, so that these words that were chosen for rhymes could not be left out. This is the prime excellence that pertains to this aspect of elocution, perhaps of greater importance than anything else.

Rhymes Must Fit Poem

I have already seen and continue to see some—too many (few are those who observe this principle or, if they do, put it into practice)—who make rhymes only for sound and think they have accomplished all that is needed, whether or not the rhymes are appropriate to the matter, significant or not. I have observed this fault not only in minor writers of little or no value but also in those who are and have been of some fame and have thought to immortalize themselves with such poems. These, either through lack of judgment or through negligence or ignorance (which even such as these do not lack), have so composed their Romances that half of the verse, including the rhymes, has no apparent significance; the rhymes are there like foreign visitors and as words that do not belong to the work but appear (as you know, I am accustomed to say) to be borrowed or rented. These are so annoying and so distasteful to a judicious reader that, whereas they ought to be pleasing and harmonious in fitting into the whole, they are only the strings of an instrument badly out of tune; though stroking them makes some sound, it is so distasteful and displeasing (lacking the rhythm, the measure, in which good harmony consists) that they cannot be listened to. This occurs in rhymes because the ear, fully expecting a final consonance that will convey the feeling harmoniously but finding it empty and inappropriate to the meaning of what it expected, is offended beyond belief. Not the ear alone but also the intellect, expecting to yield itself to rhyme and offended by its emptiness, is left without the end that it reasonably desired, to apprehend the meaning. This happens also when the poet fills up the verse with vain and insignificant words to create rhyme. This is what Horace would tell us, though he spoke of Latin composition, when he said that it was not enough for the poet to close up the verse.[95]

The composer of Romances, therefore, ought not to be a slave to rhyme and words, but (as we have always striven to do in our works) to make rhymes and words serve the thought, not vice versa. He ought to exercise all care to find words for the thoughts, not the thoughts for the words, and to use those that fit the thought, in the service of which they should be placed together; otherwise he will betray himself as a composer of little judgment.

A great difficulty inheres in so much smoothness and harmony; namely, the necessity that the rhymes of the first six verses, three and three, agree harmoniously in sound, in meaning, and in smoothness; and likewise the two that make up the last two verses of the stanza, which because of their proximity make a smoother sound than the others. Sometimes it is necessary, to make the rhymes fit, for the matter to be accompanied by foreign words, since they cannot be drawn from words that carry the matter in itself. In this respect it is necessary to employ no little genius to find rhymes that are both natural and fitting to the matter. Indeed, it is much more imperative to practice this than there is the need for the poet to see that such rhymes, though drawn from elsewhere, seem fitting to the matter and sisters to one another and placed by art, not by need or poverty of rhyme. Petrarch did this when he was faced with this necessity not only in the *Triumphs*, where he took a little more license (though not without reason, as will be made clear later) but in the canzoni and in the sonnets, where he was extremely careful, as in this sonnet:

> Non d'atra e tempestosa onda marina
> Fuggio, in porto già mai stanco Nocchiero;
> Com'io dal fosco, e torbido pensiero
> Fuggo, ove il gran desio mi sprona e inchina.[96]

Here we see that the word *inchina* was used by necessity; nevertheless, it was placed in such a way as to increase the artistry, and it seems natural there. Another example is: "ch'ogni Smeraldo havria ben vinto e stanco." It may be that *stanco* in this context is a little sharper than *inchina*, cited above. This judicious writer coped in another way with the necessity in the madrigal (if we should so name it), which begins,

> Nova angeletta sovra l'ale accorta.
> Tese fra l'herba, ond'e verde'l camino.[97]

It is clear here that all this, *ond'e verde'l camino*, drawn as an explanation from the nature of the grass, was put there to make the rhyme; but it is done so artfully that it is marvelous to see it so.

Many other examples from this most felicitous poet could

be cited; but perhaps we should discuss the stanza or ottava rima, which, so far as we know, Petrarch never wrote. Thus I shall forego the citation of further examples from him and shall show that Monsignor Bembo, whose fifty *Stanze* are regarded by judicious writers as the paragons of this kind of writing, has often written with much grace native rhymes accompanied by those borrowed from the outside, especially in the stanza that begins "Quanto in mill'anni il ciel devea mostrarne."[98] At the end of this he said:

> Fermi ne be vostri occhi un solo sguardo
> Et fugga poi (se puo) veloce o tardo.[99]

In these verses the word *tardo* is put there only to create the consonance. But *tardo* counterposed to *veloce* softens the necessity and shows it was put there artfully, not for need. If I am allowed to judge concerning this rare and novel genius whose memory I shall ever cherish and to speak freely, the first conclusion he made to this stanza is much more pleasing than the second. The first was as follows:

> Fermisi a mirar voi sol una volta
> Et fugga poi (se puo) con l'alma sciolta.[100]

It seems to me cleaner, purer, freer from the straining after an unnatural rhyme. I believe this happened because he wished to shun the similarity of rhyme sometimes put in the last stanza, and in this one also. Even if these two rhymes are similar in sound and in word, nevertheless, because of the difference in meaning, they would not be thin even though both had been put in the same stanza. But in his fifty stanzas he was so scrupulous as to be damaging to himself, as we shall show at more length below.

This same thing Ariosto did often, especially in this stanza, in the twenty-fourth canto.

> Scrive l'auttore (il cui nome mi taccio)
> Che non furo lontani una giornata
> Che per torsi Odorico quello impaccio,
> Contra ogni patto, e ogni fede data;
> Al collo di Gabrina gittò un laccio,
> Et, ch'ad un Olmo la lasciò impicata,
> Et, ch'indi a un anno (ma non dice il loco)
> Almonio a lui fece il medesimo gioco.[101]

In this stanza two phrases, *il cui nome mi taccio* and *ma non dice il loco*, are not there naturally but are brought in and put there to form the consonance; nevertheless this was made so artfully that it seems as delightful to see it thus as if it had been natural.

Forced Rhymes The judicious writer, then, ought to do similarly whenever the rhyme seems to be forced. He ought to take care not to use those which seem rented (as I have said), as are almost all those in the book I now have in hand (as you know) to revise or (to say it better) to recompose. There artificial padding is made by introducing a comparison that carries with it the rhyme needed, as Monsignor Bembo made in this stanza.

> Qual credenza d'haver senza Amor pace,
> Senza cui vita lieta huom mai non have;
> Le sante leggi sue fuggir vi face,
> Come cosa mortal si fugge, e pave?[102]

The last verse carries in it the comparison that fills out the rhyme elegantly and produces a delightfully smooth consonance, yet *pave*, which makes the consonance, is outside the word *fuggire* used before and to which it was sufficient to respond with the word *fugge*. But, since what is feared is fled from, he added *pave* to *fugge* employing transposition of the words; it is as if he had said, as a thing that *si pava, si fugge*.

Granted that Ariosto used this filling made by comparison in many places, he used it in this stanza as in the first canto.

> In dosso la coruzza, e l'elmo in testa,
> La spada al fianco, e'n braccio havea lo scudo,
> Et piu leggier correa per la foresta,
> Ch'al pallio rossa il villan mezzo nudo.[103]

The comparison or similitude as it is here carries in itself the rhyme, which gives admirable aid to the sound and the necessity. The same thing occurs when figurative speech is inserted, in which what belongs to the part is given for the whole, as Bembo did in the stanza that begins "Ond' io vi do con fe questo consiglio,"[104] where he writes:

> Vien poi, canuta il crin, severa il ciglio,
> La faticosa e debile vecchiezza.[105]

Here *canuta il crin, severa il ciglio*, employed in this figure of speech to accompany the sound of the other rhymes, gracefully relieves the necessity. This kind of figure I have also used in *The Journey of Juno to Neptune*, in stanzas that you, Messer Giovambattista, too mindful of honoring me, showed to one who, using it in his own compositions, made the invention that was solely mine to be common to him and me. This figure is seen in the following stanza:

> Altre co lor Tritoni in care danze
> Nude le braccia, e nude le mammelle,

> Empivan di timori, e di speranze
> I Dei, ch'entrati in ballo eran con elle:
> Et perche il lor disio via piu s'avanze,
> Accendean tutta via nuove fiammelle
> Co' vivi sguardi negli accesi cori,
> Ne lor giovava esser tra freddi humori.[106]

It is seen here that *nude le braccia e nude le mammelle* is introduced with figurative language to effect the smoothness and consonance of the rhyme. The same thing is done artfully in another way, namely, by interpolating a parenthesis (a figure so called by the Greeks because it breaks the sentence by being inserted in the midst of it), as Ariosto did in many places in his Romances, of which I spoke above concerning the two verse forms. I shall cite only this writer as representative of all the others I observed. This example is found in the tenth canto.

> Era ugualmente il Principe d'Anglante
> Tutto fatato, fuor ch'in una parte:
> Ferito esser potea sotto le piante,
> Ma le guardò con ogni studio & arte.
> Duro era il resto lor piu, che diamante
> (Se la fama dal ver non si diparte).[107]

This stanza clearly exhibits that the interpolation was put there solely to have a rhyme *diparte* to go along with the others. The same thing is done in the following stanza.

> Che cosi tosto, che tu aprirai gli occhi
> (Ilche indugiar però non potra molto)
> Chiaro vedrai, che tra diletti sciocchi
> Costei t'haura con sue lusinghe involto,
> Et che (per quanta gioia indi in te fiocchi)
> Sarai tra vanità vivo sepolto,
> Et morto a quella vita: laqual face,
> Che quanto Idonia dà, tutto dispiace.[108]

Besides the modes discussed, there are many and varied others, not only in the two authors cited but also in Petrarch himself, from whom the others have borrowed the mode. But since I do not wish to go further than necessary into this matter, it suffices at present to have pointed to the fountain, since I am writing to you who are able yourself, without aid, to walk confidently through these fields.

Perhaps I allowed myself, in my desire to be helpful, to be carried further than was necessary. But my reason was that this fault is now seen in writers who pay attention only to the sound of rhymes and who do not consider whether or not they fit what they write. Their crudity incites only laughter, whenever their works come under the judgment of those who strive that their works do have, I shall not say rhyme (a thing of such importance) but not one syllable that is insignificant and that does not serve the matter, if not principally for itself, at least for art and beauty. This Monsignor Bembo did by assiduous artistry. Ariosto did it more by nature than by the eager diligence put into it. Although he was indefatigable, yet he had nature so easily both in this kind of poem and in his comedies, in which he has equaled the ancient, that whoever reads them judiciously sees clearly that he owed more to nature than to art.

Nature and Art — Of these two, however, the one so needs the other that each is of little value alone. Indeed, art without nature produces such impoverished verses that they seem to have suffered for ten years from the hectic fever. Nature without art makes them like fat peasants who are of good color and health but withal have no gentility. Granted that there have been verses from the natural ear that gave them the rhythm and the endings, it must be known that these were harsh at first. This rarely occurs when art is present and the verses are revised to be perfect. So would it have ever been if nature had not been united with diligence and with the ornament of art of prudent and industrious men, who purged the verses of all which caused their unseemliness and put them in such a form that nature, aided by art, was revealed in them with admirable grace.

The works of those poets who have both nature and art for their guides cannot help but to become praiseworthy. By art I mean here not the intricacies and the entanglements of which I spoke above, which with metaphors, enigmas, and monstrosities would turn authors into alchemists; which precepts can make it appear that a man has seen and read much, but are not likely to teach; but that which gives us light, not shadow; makes our way pleasant, not painful; easy, not intricate; level, not steep; that which leads us not through briars but through flowering meadows; that which teaches us without so much tortuousness and such monstrosities of words and images. Like arranged flowers, after we have chosen them from the green fields of poesy, our compositions ought to be set in order with marvelous beauty.

To teach these things concerning words Monsignor Bembo was so diligent in our language that it seems to me I can safely put everyone who wishes to have full judgment of the nature of words and their artistic placement to reading his *Prose*, but not to the wheels of so many millstones promising us repose but whirling us around and tormenting us endlessly like new Ixions and making us miss what we would seek, as we do with no profit, in such gyres. Therefore we have to know finally (I would say this firmly to those to whom it is more pleasing to be whirled about with such ignorant leaders than to keep their feet on the ground with those who would show plainly and easily the road to good composition) that such fantasies confound our minds, fill them with vanities, and divert them from important and fruitful matters. Anyone not totally devoid of judgment can easily see that more fruit and greater profit can be drawn from their principles and that these falsities are displeasing to and avoided like wicked things by one who would grasp the art of composition.

To this another point should be added: The poet ought to pay the greatest attention in his stanzas to that part of the meaning which can be completed in two verses, so that, by two verses at a time, the reader can pause. I said two verses at a time, since, although it happens sometimes that there is a pause from one verse to another, this is not adequate because a true pause requires two rhymes called the sequence of two and two joined in the continuum of the stanza, in the same manner as the Latins used in their elegies or as Horace used in his epodes. In compositions made in this manner, Flaminio[109] did not observe this nor the admirable course of the hendecasyllabic Phalaecean[110] from verse to verse, as Catullus first did, afterward the authors of the lewd poems attributed by many to Vergil; and in our time Pontano,[111] though he is weaker in hendecasyllables that do not fit into the whole; and finally the most noble Marullo.[112] But Flaminio, handling these in the manner of the heroic, made them less smooth than nature demands for such verses, though he was most obser-

Rhythmic Principle of the Stanza

vant in language. Giacopo Acciaivoli[113] did not fall into this error, since he so united observance of the words with metrical rhythm that he succeeded not only in hendecasyllables but in every kind of lyric no less happily in the elegies than in the heroic, so well did he accommodate the ear to the measure and to the sound of the words in all kinds of verse.

Turning back to the stanza: Consisting of pairs of verses, the stanza ought to have a pause, as we have said, since this shows a purity and a natural ease in the writer and offers much beauty for his work. If this is not done, the course of the stanza is impeded and the meter becomes less smooth. So that the proof of this can be seen, I submitted two stanzas of Monsignor Bembo to the judgment of a discreet reader, of which one goes in pairs of verses with pleasing pause; the other is in the second manner; namely, that which does not quieten the reader with pairs of verses but requires him to go into the other verses for the completion of the sentence. Here is the first:

> Che giova possedar cittadi & regni,
> Et palagi habitar d'alto lavoro?
> Et servi intorno haver d'imperio degni,
> Et l'larche gravi per molto thesoro?
> Esser cantate da sublimi ingegni,
> Da porpora vestir, mangiar in oro?
> Et di bellezza appareggiar il Sole,
> Giacendo poi nel letto & fredde & sole?[114]

The other stanza:

> Questa novellamente ai padri nostri
> Spiro disio, di cui, come a Dio piacque,
> Per adornarne il mondo, & gli occhi nostri
> Bear de la sua vista, in terra nacque
> L'alta vostra beltà; ne lingua o inchiostri

Contar porria; nè vanno in mar tant' acque,
Quant' Amor da begli occhi alta & diversa
Gioia, pace, dolcezza, & gratia versa.[115]

It is apparent, if I am not deceived, that the first runs like a tranquil and beautiful stream with its course flowing smoothly, not twisted, not uproarious, not involved, and from it the ear takes great delight. The other goes on like a torrent with waves dashing and twisting together or with one weighing on the other, with an unpleasant sound. And indeed both come from the same master, not of just passable but of the highest excellence. This shows that if this adroit and judicious writer, in fifty stanzas written on an amorous and pleasing subject of marvelous beauty, with much meditation, to which he has put his hand many times, pruning them constantly, and adorning them with the highest diligence, was not able to produce works without having among them stanzas of slow and tortuous course, so much less could one manage grave and restricted matter that is not softened by another's hand, without writing hundreds and thousands of them. This also shows that it is necessary sometimes for the composer (in spite of himself) to strike against this rock, since he would rather impede the course of the stanza than the expression of the thought. Yet our Ariosto, since he was highly judicious and had an admirable natural bent for this kind of rhymes, in a great number of stanzas seldom encountered this same difficulty.

Not less to be avoided is completing or closing the meaning of the two verses of the stanza we have mentioned, so that the word which ought to complete or close the ideas falls in the first foot of another verse, even though this sometimes happens pleasantly at the turns. Nonetheless ninety times out of a hundred this position is offensive to the reader who, intent on the course and natural rhythm of the verse, feels cut off or impeded by the word that must close it to complete the meaning. As in Latin heroic verse this gives pleasing grandeur to the verse when done judiciously; so if not well done it detracts from verse in the vulgar as in the Latin it detracts from the hendecasyllabic Phalaecean (which is more like ours than any other, being also of eleven syllables) and also from the epodic. As we said above, this heroic measure of ours (the stanza has been taken as such, i.e., the heroic, and accepted by our poets) has other meter and other forms than the Latin. The grace and beauty of the Latin is that the verses do not always have their end, as far as meaning is concerned, at the end of the verse, since ending it thus causes lowness and slowness, as can be seen in the hexameters of Tibullus in the eulogy of Messala.[116]

In contrast, the epithalamium of Catullus on the marriage of Peleus and Thetis, also in hexameters, shows how much magnificance may be given to the verses by knowing how to vary the measures and to provide a pause for one verse sometimes in the beginning of the others, sometimes in the middle, as is required by the matters at hand, and by grace and majesty. Our poets, as to this device, would always have the end at the junction of verse with verse and would not let one run into the other, breaking the measure, as we have said. Examples of how such a position may be unpleasing appear more than once in the same *Stanze* of Monsignor Bembo, as in the stanza beginning "O quanto è dolce, perche Amor lo stringa,"[117] in the two verses:

> Saper, come due volti un sol depinga
> Color, come due voglie regga un freno.[118]

Another example appears in the stanza that begins "Cosi voi vi trovate altrui cercando,"[119] in these two verses:

> Dunque perche di voi ponete in bando
> Amor: se son di tanto ben radici
> Le sue fiamme?[120]

One can easily recognize that the word *color* in the first two verses and the word *Amor* in the second two greatly hinder the pleasantly natural course of the verse.¶

Now, turning to the permitted necessity: When it really leads the writer to a breaking of this sort, to which (as we said) he is more often led than is necessary for the pleasing quality of the stanzas, he will employ it much less badly if he uses the relative pronoun, as in Petrarch's sonnet "L'alto & novo miracol," when he said:

> Vuol, ch'i depinga a chi no'l vide, & mostri,
> Amor che'n prima la mia lingua sciolse.[121]

In this sonnet *Amor*, placed at the beginning of the [second] verse, depends on the meaning of the first verse; nevertheless, by means of the relative which follows, it has much smoother jointure than the word *color* in Monsignor Bembo's stanza [No. 45]. Similar jointure is seen in the word *donne* in the sonnet:

> Liete, pensose, accompagnate, & sole
> Donne, che ragionando ite per via,[122]

where the relative softens the harshness of *donne* placed at the beginning of the verse. It will also be less displeasing if this is done with two or three words rather than one, and if the pause goes as far as the middle of the verse or a little short. The course so broken becomes less ungraceful as can be seen in the last verse cited in Bembo's stanza, where the break, made with three words *Le sue fiamme*, is much less offensive than the other two.

To derive a general rule from this: However often the necessity will occur (and one sees it occurs often), if the grammatical construction of the verb or of the relative or of the adjunct or another similar device is so employed that words are not placed after when they may be placed before, it will be tolerable enough, as if in Bembo's stanza it had been written:

> Saper come un color solo dipinga
> Due volti.

If this cannot be done with two or three words, the word in which the meaning must be placed will carry with it less unseemliness if it is composed of more than two syllables; if composed of more than three it will be even more graceful.

One should know indeed that often the meaning is not only not completed in a pair of verses but at times it is not completed in the whole stanza when the meaning is carried over into another stanza (as we see also occurred often in Petrarch in the tercets and quatrains of his sonnets, and in the terza rimas, which naturally, as sets of three verses, would have their pause even though the meaning may go beyond them). If this is done neatly (though the more rarely, the better), it is not inappropriate, for the writer's talent holds the reader's mind in suspension so that he lets himself be carried willingly beyond the eight verses to hear the end of the thought begun in the second stanza; but for all that, this does not imply that the part of the meaning each stanza comprises ought not to be distributed in two verses at a time, as we said. The broken jointure displeases and, if not put in its place in two verses when the meaning of one stanza passes into the second, does not supply an end in the manner mentioned.

To add to this ease and smoothness and pause in the meanings, the sentence of the last two verses of the stanza ought to be wrought with felicitous course and great smoothness and appropriateness of rhymes, for if the reader or hearer fully expects an end, his recognition of it is pleasanter, he pauses more voluntarily, and he is more eager to hear the other stanzas. In this, along with the delight that the poet gives, he is shown to have good judgment in knowing how to capture the reader's mind with delightful adroitness and admirable skill, so that it seems to be done naturally without any art. If these last two verses embrace a certain charming and wonderful *sententia* appropriate for common actions, it enters wonderfully into the reader's or hearer's mind, so effective is the sound of the rhymes, so delighted with it are the ear and the mind.

Besides this, the writer of Romances ought also to be careful to avoid the repetition of the same words in any one stanza, since such practice annoys the reader and shows the writer's poverty, except when it is done to adorn or to add force and vigor to the meaning of the verse, as we see Ariosto did when he said: "Eran rivali, eran di fe diversi"; and elsewhere, when speaking of Ariodante after the death of Polinesso: "Di tal bonta, di tal valor splendea."[123] Repetition made very nobly can also be seen in the same author, when Ruggiero converses with the myrtle tree, saying:

Avoidance of Repetition

> Per quella bella donna io ti prometto;
> Per quella, c'ha di me la miglior parte.[124]

Repetition such as this is graceful and forceful and almost natural in this kind of composition. I am not speaking therefore of the laudable repetition of words well known in all poetic composition in this language and greatly ornamental to the verses, provided it is done in its place and time with discreet judgment, but of that which becomes tedious, showing little judgment and poverty in the writer. The sort showing little judgment is exemplified in Pulci in his *Morgante*, in which many stanzas often begin with the same word. This annoys a reader incredibly.

As for poverty of thought, this is exhibited abundantly by those who seek nothing but to bring a verse to an end. I judge it excessive to cite here the examples that are indeed in abundance in the pages of those who, scribbling on papers, write neither to themselves nor to others. This sometimes occurs in the most distinguished writers, though, indeed, they use idle and repeated words only with great judgment. Granted that the repetition of unworthy words is to be avoided in any use of words, their repetition in rhymes ought to be studiously avoided, for these more than all the others are weighed and more than all prove to be outside good usage. I do not say this because the same rhyming words cannot be used, as Petrarch did in the sonnet "Quando io son tutto volto in quella parte";[125] and Monsignor Bembo in the stanza "Il qual errando in questa e in quella parte,"[126] where it is seen that *parte* and *luce* make the eight rhymes of the sonnet, and *parte* and *seno* make the six of the stanza; in both, the rhymes came forth quite felicitously, through the varied signification of the words *parte, luce, seno*. But I say that the repetition of rhymes ought to be avoided when they are in the same stanza or in other stanzas when they are close together or when one follows the other. He who could always do this without fault, without danger of affectation (which ought to be avoided at all costs) or harshness or bungling would be eminently praiseworthy. Monsignor Bembo practiced this rule so prudently that in all his fifty stanzas no rhyme is repeated, though similar ones are to be found so close that at times only three stanzas intervene. This is why he ended this stanza less felicitously: "Quanto in mill'anni il ciel devea mostrarne,"[127] as we said above. But as the avoidance of repeated rhymes was easy for Bembo in that he managed them smoothly in a small number of stanzas, it is difficult for one who must compose hundreds and thousands of rhymes to sustain a long work, as witness Ariosto in his Romances. This happens because the matter of two or three stanzas sometimes carries within it the same rhymes appropriate to the subject; the writer, wishing to express the thought with other words, either needs to change the meaning or to say it less gracefully.

Let me give an example of this in Ariosto himself, who in the first edition of his Romances (speaking of Sacripante as he ran affectionately toward Angelica) had left this stanza of the first canto so written:

> Pieno di dolce affetto & riverente
> Alla sua donna, alla sua donna corse.
> Lo raccolse ella piu cortesemente
> Che non faria se fusse in India forse:
> Al regno di suo padre in Oriente,
> Seco havendo costui l'animo torse;
> Subito in lei si aviva la speranza.
> Di presto riveder sua ricca stanza.

But afterward, in the final edition, which he completed just before he died (indeed not long after he had published the *Furioso* in the form we now have it, he was afflicted with a most serious illness that gave him great pain and was under the care of the most Excellent M. Giovanni Manardi, who went to comfort him in his incurable illness; so this happy spirit departed this life, to whom our age and language and the most noble Este family and our native land altogether are no less indebted than were the former age, the Latin language, Octavian, and Mantua to the good Vergil), offended by the proximity of the same and similar rhymes in the present stanza and in a good many others, he left it written thus:

> Pieno di dolce & d'amoroso affetto
> Alla sua donna, alla sua diva corse,
> Che con le braccia al collo il tenne stretto,
> Quel, ch'al Catai non havria fatto forse
> Al patrio Regno, al suo, natio ricetto,
> Seco havendo costui l'animo torse;
> Subito in lei si aviva la speranza
> Di tosto riveder sua ricca stanza.[128]

From this, one may see clearly that the rhymes of the first stanza were those which ought to express the thought, and that those of the second were forced. The word *riverente* shows the grandeur of the lady and the respect Sacripante had for her; however, aroused by love, he nevertheless esteemed the lady's regality. *Lo raccolse ella piu cortesemente* shows Angelica's modesty accompanied by the courtesy she should show admirably to Sacripante in her need, by whom she hoped to be relieved. This stanza puts this courteous act gently before the eyes, whereas in the second stanza, the line "Che con le braccia al collo il tenne stretto" is full of unseemly lasciviousness and thus obscures its effect, making courtesy an unchaste act. Similarly the verse "Al regno di suo padre in Oriente" moves lightly and agilely without an inappropriate or insignificant word, whereas the other, "Al patrio Regno, al suo natio ricetto," moves less lightly and half of it is a forced rhyme, since *al suo natio ricetto* (perhaps others would not put up with subtleties) is none other than *al patrio Regno*, and the word *patrio* is not a word of the language. Perhaps, as he changed *presto* of the last verse to *tosto*, it would have been better to leave the stanza as it was, not changing to the word *diva*, which refers to the beloved lady, not to her after her death, as Petrarch did very neatly when he said in the second capitolo of *The Triumph of Death*: "Come non conosch'io l'alma mia diva?"[129] This occurs again in the sonnet that begins "Quel sempre acerbo, & honorato giorno,"[130] which he composed on the life of his lady, in this verse: "Facean dubbiar se mortal donna, o diva."[131] The word *diva* does not signify Madonna Laura but a goddess or a divine being, as if he had said, I doubt whether she was a human woman or a divine being.***

Leaving this subject, let us now consider whether the poet can change tenses when the quality of the discourse or necessity (which is without law) raises the question, as did Ariosto in this stanza. Having said,

Shifting of Tense

> Al patrio Regno, al suo natio ricetto,
> Seco havendo costui l'animo torse;

he then said: "Subito in lei si aviva la speranza," where logically the tense should be *avivò*. In the same way he did this frequently in various places, especially when he said of Orlando's fury:

> Fu all'hora per uscir di sentimento
> Si tutto in preda del dolor si lascia;

where according to tense, he should not have said *lascia*, but *lasciò*; then having said *lascia*, he should have said, in the verse "Caduto gli era sopra il petto il mento," not *caduto gli era* but *gli cade*, in the present tense. Indeed, after so much revision, he left these verses written as we now read them. It seemed to him (as also to me) that the poet of the Romances could without censure take this license, as the Greeks first took it, then the Latins, and the Tuscans also, as witness the many examples of it in Dante, Petrarch, and others who have written with praise in this language. From the authority of these I refrain now from filling these pages with what is altogether clear in itself.

Justifiable Repetition Turning therefore to our discussion, I say that it is better to use similar rhymes and the same in two neighboring stanzas if by not using them violence is done to the total expression of the subject, with rhymes foreign to it. Ariosto tended to use nearness and similarity of rhyme in various places in his poem rather than force the thought. But passing over other matters (to avoid undue length), I shall be content to cite these two successive stanzas with rhymes sometimes similar, at other times identical.

> Ruggier, che vide il Comite, e il Padrone
> Et gli altri abandonar con fretta il legno,
> Come senza arme si trovò, in giupone
> Campare in quel battel fece disegno,
> Ma lo trovò si carco di persone,
> Et tante venner poi, che l'acque il segno
> Passaro in guisa, che per troppo pondo,
> Con tutto il carco andò il legnetto al fondo.

> Del mare al fondo, & seco trasse quanti
> Lasciaro a sua speranza il maggior legno.
> All hor s'udì con dolorosi pianti
> Chiamar soccorso dal celeste Regno:
> Ma quelle voci andaro poco inanti,
> Che venne il mar pien d'ira, & di disdegno,
> Et subito occupò tutta la via,
> Onde il lamento, e il flebil grido uscia.[132]

I nevertheless praise ways in which this propinquity can be avoided, especially with rare rhymes like *imago*, *Argo*, *Mauro*, *vespe*, *Mancipio*, *Lembo*, *empio*, and such others, which being few and little used, smack too much of the obsolete or foreign, if too frequent. For these and for others at least eight or ten stanzas would be required to intervene between identical rhymes, so that no page of ten stanzas would have the same rhymes. To speak truly, such propinquity, especially of rare rhymes, offends too much, except when a judicious reader recognizes that it is neither the writer's poverty nor his carelessness but his judgment and the character of the subject that makes them occur thus for him. For it is better (as I said just now) effectively to express a thought with similar or identical rhymes than to narrate it with little effectiveness merely to avoid similitude or roughness or harshness. It is true that when necessary (as it is often to anyone who would not mingle or twist the thoughts from the straight and graceful), similar rhymes ought to be used even among the ten stanzas already mentioned. It is good, if possible, not to use them in the same number nor of the same kind, as we see Petrarch did not only in his *Triumphs* but in the three canzoni on eyes,[133] which, though on the same subject, do not have identical rhymes, and those similar are of diverse kinds and numbers. Bembo does the same thing in the canzoni of the last book of the *Asolani*. I do not approve, therefore, of the credulous diligence of those who would have no canto without any repetition or similarity of rhyme (although to show that this is not impossible, I have written a set of a hundred or more stanzas in which no rhyme was repeated). It is not necessary, further, because this useless requirement would freeze the warmth of the composer and would impose on him undue labor which, even when endured, would nonetheless give him little praise. For there would be therein so much asperity, impropriety, distortion of meaning, and harshness of language (it could never be done otherwise because of the begged rhymes) that it would be clearly better to run the risk of similar or identical consonance than to be involved in such futile and profitless efforts.

Leaving everyone to his own opinion, we should note also that the poet should avoid the repetition of rhyming words in verses that follow the rhyme. Nor should there be put in these sequent lines words that conform to the consonance of the rhymes, because the hearing of sounds out of place and time is made needlessly unpleasing. If there is sometimes need to do so, as will happen, one should take heed that this word does not fall in the midst of the verse or on an accented syllable, since this is very offensive to the ear; and if it does so fall, the word that follows should not begin with a vowel different from that of the word agreeing with the rhyme, so that, in eliding, the last vowel of the word that would make the consonance is not heard and so does not cause discord. Even though this may occur right on the accented syllables, it will not be out of keeping in whatever place it is employed neatly; on the contrary, it will be with much pleasure.†††

The poet ought also to take much care not to use words *Effective*
that make the verse slow and take boldness and liveliness *Diction*
from it without which the heroic will remain without
praise. For this reason some words are often put into the
verse whole and thus are without the last vowel whenever
they are not of the first syllable or of the penultimate, and
whenever a word beginning with a consonant follows them,
such as *cagione, erano, pensiero, alcuno, pure, buono, meno,
uno, tale, qualle, fuori, essere,* and almost all the other in-
finitives of the verbs, especially if they are found on the
accented syllable. If these and similar whole words are
put in the verse in the way we have described, they gen-
erally make the verse sluggish. I shall give no other ex-
amples of this, leaving everyone to prove it in his own
experience.

If, therefore, great necessity does not force us (there is
sometimes need to obey it against our will), we ought
always, in the course of the verse (when none of the situa-
tions mentioned exist) following the consonants, to use
them without the last vowel. There are those who think
that these always make for sluggishness—*lei, altrui, lui, voi,
poi,* and others like them—whenever the last syllable, which
comprises the last two letters of the word, does not elide
with the following vowel of another word. But they may
be mistaken. Granted that this may be true at times, it
is not always true, as there are many examples of it in
Petrarch and other good writers; indeed, many times such
syllables do not elide with the following vowel, especially
where those usually of one syllable become two, and only

the last elides with that following; the verse is more beautiful and smoother than if both are elided. Since this notion is fixed in the minds of many people, to show that what I said is not without reason, I shall cite examples of the major Tuscans, some of which are in these verses. "L'una di lui, & ei dell'altra gode . . . ." "Teme di lei, ond'io son fuor di speme . . . ." "Iphi, ch'amando altrui in odio s'ebbe . . . ." "Hisiphile vien poi, & duolsi anch'ella . . . ." "Quand'in voi adivien, che gli occhi giri . . . ."[134]

I could cite many other examples like these, which we encounter frequently in one or another of the good poets. But because it is quite true that this practice sometimes causes languidness, a definite rule for it cannot be given; I shall therefore leave it to the writer's judgment. Whenever he perceives that the retaining of last syllables has caused sluggishness, he ought to see to it that they elide, and that the verse retains its life and rhythm. What I say of the words mentioned I say also of *ne, ma, chi,* and other words of one syllable which often do not elide, as in these examples in Petrarch: "Ne ovra da polir con la mia lima," and "Vissimi, che ne lor, ne altri offesi . . ."; "Ma io saro sotterra in secca selva . . ."; "Poi che seppi, chi eran piu sicuro . . . ."[135]

The same happens with words of one syllable which have to be accented, such as *si, fu, pero, piu, di* (meaning day), and others like them, all of which Petrarch often used without elision gracefully and with no distortion.

> Se si alto pon gir mie stanche rime
> Pero al mio parer non gli fu honore;

as it is in the better texts:

> Con piu altri dannati a simil sorte
> Pero che di & notte indi m'invita.[136]

So also Dante, who wrote before him, often practicing this, slowed up the course of the verse and made it quite languid, offending more often with this fault than is fitting for a judicious poet. Boccaccio did likewise in his *Teseide* and in the rhymes of his *Ameto*; in these two works he showed how far was his nature from gentle smoothness and from the rhythm of the verse. Often also the syllables *di, me, te, se* do not elide, especially at the beginnings of verses; nevertheless the verse comes out not sluggish but sonorous and smooth. I refrain from examples of these words and many others like them, for they occur frequently in famous poets.‡‡‡

Granted that for the elegance and dignity of the verse, it is necessary to study words diligently so that the choice of them may always be discriminating, in these compositions it should be stressed. Nevertheless, that the law for this kind of poetry is not so strict as to forbid words not included in the books of the famous ancient writers, indeed words in everyday usage, chosen from common speech by the judgment of whoever wishes to use them. Since this is a living language, written and spoken everywhere by the noblest writers and by gentlemen and noblemen, we should commit a great wrong if we should limit ourselves to the words of two or three authors who in ancient times wrote with distinction in certain particular works, resolving to use only the words of the dead and to avoid those that everywhere serve us in expressing our thought day by day. Neither Petrarch nor Boccaccio in the *Decameron* used *soccesso, occasione, difficulta, sesso, discorso, scena, rivale, personaggi, naufragio, steccato, lizza, imbelle, corazze, starna, stendardo, strisciare, inetto, causa, camaglio, ruggine, rugginoso, prudenza, trasferire,* and other such words so numerous as to be almost infinite; nevertheless, the usage of today makes them not only tolerable but esteemed and full of grace. Although I know that as the years give authority to men, so they give it to words of the ancient writers; nevertheless, heeding what Horace said of the Latin language when it was in common use by the Latins and the Romans, that it is drawn not only from books, as is done today, but also from the nurses' milk,[137] I would say that the words of the aforesaid authors will die out, as indeed many have, and others will be born in their place; words accepted into usage by the authority of the writer will become respectable and will express thoughts with more brilliance than could those of the ancient writers which are already discontinued. There are examples of these by those who write and discourse, among them Bembo, in both his verse and his prose, to whom this language owes much as having been revived by him and distinctively enriched in prestige.

It is true, nevertheless, that I do not commend those who in trying to write with a certain censurable license not only introduce new words contrary to rule but also use those already permitted by rule without reason, a fault especially of some Tuscans who think that because they were born in that region and under that sky where this language had its best origin (so truly fortunate and not to be misused) they are licensed to write and speak without any law. Instead, I insist that anything taken *de novo* and put into use be always restricted by the regulations and laws given to this language by the better judges, who drew them from the good writers and from a true picture of the speech and confirmed them by their authority. I see this observed by those Tuscans who think (and with reason) that license takes away the value of their language and are grateful to those who, according to the authority of the best writers, have summoned it to observe the rules now prevailing. They have deemed that without this, it could not be called a language; on the contrary, writing and speaking in it without such laws and such acceptance of them—either taught by those who wrote about them or observed in the excellent writers—would rather be at random and by a sort of habit than by reason. Monsignor della Casa[138] is a good example, as his learned and respected works bear witness, in which I find no defect except that they are few and too rarely come into my hands. Such is the noble and learned Cavalcanti[139] as witness the judgment he gives on other men's writings, especially in his highly regarded *Rhetoric*, written in our speech with such excellence that our language in this respect does not need to envy the Greek or the Latin. Such is Varchi,[140] for though he shows his genius and ability in all his works, he makes them clearest especially in his pastoral poems, in which noble spirits in our language do not fail to find the simplicity of Theocritus and the maturity of Vergil.

But, to return to where we left off: The law of writing Romances is not so strict as not to permit more license in words than appears in sonnets and canzoni. The scope and gravity of the matter require this latitude (if the thoughts are not to be crippled), but, as I have said, this latitude needs regulation. Petrarch clearly showed this in his *Triumphs*. I prefer in this connection not to discuss Dante, since through either the fault of his time or his own nature he took such liberties that his license became vice. It seems to me, therefore, that the painter worked very artfully who, endeavoring in a beautiful picture to

Greater Freedom i Diction in Romances

show us the qualities in the writings of these two poets, imagined both in a green and flowering meadow painted on the hill of Helicon; in Dante's hand he put a sickle, which the poet (with his clothing girded up to the knee) swung around and around, going about cutting every plant he came to. The painter represented Petrarch behind Dante, clad in senatorial garments, choosing the fine plants and lovely flowers; all this was intended to show the license of the former and the critical judgment of the latter. Though Petrarch was scrupulous in the use of words, in his *Triumphs* he put words and rhymes that were not in his *Canzoniere*. These were not quite innovations but were drawn from common usage and used with meanings and accents other than in his *Canzoniere*. Since Petrarch was most judicious and composed his *Triumphs* when his judgment had already become wise with age, it cannot be said that he did this because of his lack of judgment but because of the character of the subject. He conformed to the authority of Aristotle and Horace in their *Poetics*, which allow the epic poet to use new words and to alter them somewhat from the common usage, as Homer did in Greek and Vergil in Latin. They not only did this but also introduced obsolete and barbarous words to fit them to the thought and render it more effective in writing. Since a single word would not create such an effect, it was necessary to innovate or to deviate somewhat from the accepted usage in order to avoid expressing their thoughts less effectively.§§§

I do not wish now to give examples of innovations from the stanzas of the two authors cited because they are apparent even to those who read either of them casually; so I shall not cite any specifically. But I shall cite an example of those who deviate somewhat, only to show that they would rather yield to a word that is not in common use than to force their thoughts.

It is seen that Monsignor Bembo, a most scrupulous and diligent writer of verses freed from forced rhymes out of common use (as indeed Petrarch used *Tibro* instead of *Tebro* in the *Triumph of Chastity*), used in his stanzas *vice* in place of *vece*, in the manner of Dante. In fact he said in the stanza beginning:

> Come a cui vi donate, si disdice
> Sed egli a voi di se si rende avaro:
> Cosi voi donne a quei, che vi hanno in vice
> Di Sole a la lor vita dolce & chiaro.[141]

And he composed only fifty stanzas. He did likewise in his *Asolani*, in the canzone "Si rubella d'Amor ne si fugace."[142] In the first stanza of this he used *trezza* to effect, at the beginning of that verse, the consonance with the other stanzas, all of which likewise have, at the beginning of the fourth verse, a rhyme of three syllables which ends in *ezza*, as he has one which ends from stanza to stanza in *ella*, in the third verse, which effects the consonance with the others in every fifth syllable, following the order of the canzone of Petrarch beginning "Verdi panni sanguigni, oscuri, o persi."[143] Bembo made his like this one, as we also made one that may be read in our *Fiamme*, which we composed as the best that the youthful age in which it was written allowed us. Similarly Monsignor [Bembo], in his *Asolani*, yielded to the example of Dante, with the word *fame* in a plural sense, and said *fami* in this verse:

> Di pascer le gran fami
> Che in si lungo digiuno Amor mi dai.[144]

This is in the canzone of the second book, which begins "Se'l pensier, che m'ingombra,"[145] a word I do not find used by other good authors after Dante; nevertheless, I have accepted and used it by the authority of so noble a master, as I have also used (in conformity with the common daily usage) *sempio* for *semplice* or *sciocco*, and *ostri* in a plural sense, though this word Petrarch used only in the singular.

Ariosto also took this license in many places, especially when in the twenty-third canto he used *vase* instead of *vaso*, in the stanza beginning "L'impetuosa doglia entro rimase;"[146] and when he used *ugna* for *unghia* in the stanza beginning "Il primo giorno & l'ultimo che pugna."[147] In my judgment Ariosto did much better to use with a little more license than custom allowed these words that were not in Canto XXV of the first edition and revised in the XXVIIIth of the last: "Tremo Parigi, & torbidossi Senna":[148] *Ebra, latebra, Ginebra*; in their place he put *grido, lido, nido*; although the last vowels may be more frequent and made softer by use, the first rhymes, in fact, were more significant and more appropriate to the subject of the stanza in putting a din and uproar in the ears of the hearer and in the mind of the reader. Since this can be seen clearly, I shall not be irksome here in including both stanzas, since the discerning reader can judge for himself. The first is as follows:

>   Tremò Parigi & torbidossi Senna
>   A la terribil voce di quell'Ebra:
>   Ribombò il suon fin a la selva Ardenna
>   Si che lasciar le fiere ogni latebra:
>   Udiron l'Alpe e'l monte di Gebenna,
>   E il lago di Costanza & di Ginebra:
>   Rodano & Sona udì, Garona e il Rheno:
>   Si strinsero le madri i figli al seno.

This is the second:

> Tremò Parigi & torbidossi Senna
> All'alta voce, a quello horribil grido,
> Ribombò il suon fin alla selva Ardenna,
> Si, che lasciar tutte le fiere il nido,
> Udiro l'Alpe, e il monte di Gebenna,
> Di blaia, d'Arli, & di Roano il lido.
> Rhodano, & Sona udì, Garona, e il Rheno:
> Si strinsero le madri i figli al seno.[149]

These latter rhymes, as I said, were softer; but the former were more appropriate and significant in the grand effect they carry in themselves, in the meaning of the words and their harshness; since, as Quintilian teaches us, atrocious and terrible things should be written with sharp words like *Ebra, latebra, Ginebra*, not with soft words like *lido, grido, nido*.[150] This occurred in Ariosto not only in these words but in many others; sometimes changes were made to obey the rules of the language which came into being after the edition of his *Furioso*; at other times to please himself he revised, often with less brilliance for his work, as I have observed in many places by comparing the last version with the first, stanza by stanza, and by noting (as I have already discussed with you) not only the variation itself but the reason why some of the variations and changes are better, others worse; and, in fact, I have intended to collect all of them in a little book, as a short time ago I assembled in a few verses a discourse on the stanza "Pieno di dolce affetto, et riverente," so that this could be read for the common good of the studious; but many pursuits turned me aside from it. Perhaps at another time when I have more leisure, I shall carry out what I intended to do; or you who are less occupied than I will do so.

Now to pass on to the other admonitions concerning elocution: One ought to consider carefully the things that convey in themselves rapidity, so that flowing, brisk words may be used, such as *veloce, velocisissimo, velocissimamente*, and to match them with others that together they enter into the verse, so that the metrical rhythm may be designed for rapidity. For slowness, there are words with a contrasting effect, such as *tarde, lenti, pigre, nighitose*. Examples of two of these are in this sonnet of Petrarch: "Mie venture al venir son tarde, & pigre,"[151] where it is seen that this verse is quite slow; on the contrary, this other: "Et poi al fuggir son più lievi che Tigre,"[152] runs so briskly that it properly flits by and vanishes before the judicious reader's eyes. For cheerfulness, lovely, light, resonant, and smooth words should be used, as did Petrarch in the sonnet "Erano i capei d'oro a l'aura sparsi,"[153] and in the sonnet "Già fiammegiava l'amorosa stella,"[154] and in the sonnet "Dodici donne honestamente lasse,"[155] and in many other places in his *Canzoniere*; and in the sad ones the sorrowfully perturbed converges with the melancholy, as the same poet wrote in various places in reference to his lady's death, especially when he said in the canzone beginning "Che debb'io far, che mi consigli amore?"[156] This is entirely of wretchedness and grief, as is expressed wonderfully in the conclusion of this canzone, when he said:

> Canzon mia no, ma pianto:
> Per te non fa di star fra gente allegra
> Vedova, sconsolata, in vesta negra.[157]

And the canzone of the six visions has an example of the light and the doleful conveyed wonderfully. For grave effects, the words are forceful which have the sound of *m*, as is seen in this verse of the first sonnet: "Di me medismo meco mi vergogno;"[158] and the sonnet "Mentre che il cor da gli amorosi vermi."[159] Not without reason was this selected by Monsignor Bembo[160] as a model of sweetness and of affecting graveness, which is almost always a companion to that effect. Although there are some who grant Petrarch little judgment in this particular, to them one only answers that they have the ears of Midas. Even if in this sonnet there is the *r* (a letter as frequent in our language as the *b* and the *q* are rare), by nature clamorous, it is managed with such grace and judgment that it becomes, by means of its company and by the admixture of the other letters, soft and less harsh. Thus the grave effect is conveyed gracefully. So well did Petrarch know the force of the *m* mingled with the *r* in the expression of love that he undertook to display it with affectionate seriousness in this sonnet in which he was content not only that four of the eight rhymes end their last syllable in *m* and the penultimate in *r* but also that in the six [sestet] two, *marmo* and *disarmo*, end the same way.

But, not to multiply words and examples: The writer ought generally to be very careful that the words be proportionate to the matter they are to convey and to be thus joined and mingled. He should pay attention to the effects of the words—slowness, harmony, humbleness, exaltation, loudness, smoothness, gravity—so that it will be apparent immediately that if the thought had been conveyed with other words of other arrangement, the poem would have come forth less seriously, less beautifully, and less effectively. In fact, the position chosen for any word is of no little importance, since the smoothness of speech, on which the poet must concentrate in order to impress on the hearers' or readers' minds the ways and emotions of life, consists in the order and arrangement of words chosen judiciously. He will be judged, then, as to whether the order and disposition is well managed, whether the words hold such a place that if a conjunction is changed, even though the sense may remain, the verse will lose its grace and sweetness or will be less beautiful and felicitous. On this matter no rule can be given; since it depends wholly on practice, it will suffice us to have stressed what ought to be warned about. But the composer's diligent study will be put to work, as we have said, whenever he will not be content with spitting out his verses but will take them under mature consideration, removing the words that do not please him and putting others in their place. With the measure of the sound and the rhythm (the judicious ear is well accustomed to such harmony) will go such weighing and changing of words that he will see them placed in such a way that they can satisfy not only him but whoever will read judiciously. Those who are content with their verses as they first fall from the pen can never please. Believe me, Messer Giovambattista, holding back verses and weighing them diligently according to the rules of style is one of the better things a diligent writer can do. The pen is often much more helpful to compositions when it condemns and corrects what is written than when it first writes these compositions. The one comes from the warmth of composing, the other from judgment.

Art Should Seem like Nature Though one cannot write well without the most intense diligence and great labor (nature has not arranged for excellence to issue from us without labor), nonetheless the writer ought to strive with the utmost effort, not so that the hard work on the composition will be visible, but so that the work will appear to be done naturally. Among the Latins, Vergil knew how to do this so well that, although he put much labor on his poem, as if he formed his verses as the she-bear shapes her cubs with her tongue; and considering the time he took in composing his *Aeneid* and the number of verses (he did not write a few of them, as the other writers say, but hardly two a day), he so concealed his labor from the world that it seems the words nevertheless fell naturally from his pen with marvelous arrangement. Neither Statius nor Valerius Flaccus knew how to do this, for the works of these two authors are very rough and far from any natural vein. Quintilian said, however, that the Latin language lost much by Flaccus' death.[161] Statius, it is true, realizing the error, freed himself from the ones he made in his *Thebaid*, which he said he had tortured with much revising for twelve whole years;[162] he showed better judgment in his *Achilliad*, coming closer in it to the natural than to the laborious mode of writing. But the span of more than a thousand years had given such authority and reputation to these two authors that Politian and Strozza the Younger[163] tried to write hexameters in the style of Flaccus rather than of Vergil. And Pontano, a fine poet of exquisite judgment, and Sannazaro, devoted to the study and imitation of Vergil, often did not avoid the grammatical constructions and the numbers of Statius. They did so either because of the quality of that heaven under which all three were born or because of the authority they wished to give with their compositions to the numbers of that poet in their country who had written earlier than they.

Ovid, on the contrary, allowed too much to nature and followed too much his own sweet will, so that his works are like fields of the greenest corn, overly soft and luxuriant. This has caused him to appear more ingenuous than profound, more licentious than attentive to law, more copious than diligent. This is not to be seen in Lucretius, who though he had nature for a guide, nevertheless so tempered it with judgment in those times when Roman poetry was little less than crude, that even in lascivious subjects he showed himself grave. Like Lucretius in following nature was Count Matheo [Boiardo] in our language, who, although he was a little rougher than beauty of composition required, was, however, the first who put his foot on the good road and taught others to walk in it laudably.¶¶¶

But to return to those who concealed the labor they put into composition: Petrarch among the Tuscans merited this praise, as is apparent in his verses. Although he revised, revised again, corrected, and polished them, they remained easy and soft in spite of that. In order to achieve this essential skill (nothing seems easier to do, but it then proves exceedingly difficult for him who tries to use it against the vice of childishness), the writer of Romances must strive so that the ordering and composition of his verses be such that his stanzas seem one piece of prose, not, I say, as to numbers, because verse has one rhythmical movement, prose another, but as to the order and ease of the discourse. The verses ought to be such, in regard to the order of construction, that words that ought to be put behind are not put before, and vice versa. It should be done so that the verses exhibit no forced construction, no distortion; so that articles, adjuncts, adverbs hold their proper position. Although the poet (in order to adapt himself to the difficulty of the rhymes, perhaps greater in this language than that of syllables in Greek and Latin) is sometimes allowed to vary this order, putting words forward or back as is most convenient for him; nevertheless, he ought to be wary that this necessity does not become habit. The poet should not practice this so much that he seems to be a barbarian writing Italian, that his work shows a great deal of laborious writing, without a trace of nature, much like a thread full of knots which, no matter how long it is drawn out, will not be fit for good weaving. Into this vice have fallen and are falling nearly all those who, since Ariosto, have written Romances. Generally the reason for this has been their lack of judgment in placing rhymes; because lacking this, they try to make the consonance and in so doing they so distort the words that their work comes out lamed by infinite twisting of the meaning, indeed full of useless, insignificant words. This is rarely seen in Ariosto, and then more by necessity than expedience. To complete our discussion about hiding one's labor, I say that Ariosto himself has a marvelously natural ease in concealing all his work, so that not a sign of it remains, even though he spent more than thirty years in composing and revising his work.

Nevertheless the writer ought to be alert that this ease we are talking about does not so divert him from seriousness and sententiousness that he remains childish, if the stanzas be of sweet sound but of little meaning, without which the numbers, the sound, and other things we have mentioned do not function. All these are in relation to happy expressions of thought; when they lack the purpose for which they are considered, they are quite empty and, though they may appear beautiful, are worth nothing. I remember reading about eight hundred stanzas by a writer of our time of some note, which seemed to be gathered from the flowering gardens of poesy, so beautiful were they, stanza after stanza; but altogether they were so empty of sense that they seemed to have been born in the land of childhood. The author, having concentrated entirely on delight, which is born of brilliance and the choice of words, neglected entirely the dignity and advantage that comes from meaning. He who would write could do nothing worse. If one has to err in one of the two, he had better please with rough words than with sonorous and delicate words that give sweet sound and no fruit.

In Dante and Cino there are often examples of those which please without sweetness; and those with sweetness are often empty and too soft. Petrarch is midway between the two extremes; by blending the serious with the sweet, he excelled in both. Emptiness is the general fault of those who are exercised only with words and have not devoted themselves to the study of philosophy, without which all the works turn out to be empty, because it is like a spring from which flow all the streams of things which give to renowned writers the subjects of their compositions; as those have said whom anyone desiring knowledge of it should read from beginning to end. But I shall only linger to say (since indeed I have gone to excess in this discussion) that the happy geniuses, nourished by the milk of this great madonna, ought to guard against being damaged by the abundance that flows from this fountain. Just as rich fields produce not only the grain sowed in them but also weeds so noxious that they often kill it if the tillage is lacking; so also, with the sprouting of the seeds of the disciplines; in the fields of the minds other things spring up which, if left to flourish unrecognized by the writers, injure their compositions rather than help them at all. Therefore, as the diligent laborer in the fields uproots the weeds, which injure the grain, so he who would write should know how to choose judiciously from the good that philosophy has given and to take out all that could damage his work, leaving only what is pleasing, fittingly serious, and apt to make his work lively and splendid. I said pleasant as well as serious because he ought to take care (as we said above when we discussed the introduction of customs) not to be trapped in harsh, unpleasant, melancholic seriousness in both what is excessively repulsive and what is facilely immature. Just as the orator is heard with gravity, so the poet is heard with sweetness; if this is lacking in him, he remains unpleasing.

It is even more indecorous for the one writing to show himself a philosopher, to neglect poetic grace and beauty, and, concentrating on words and recondite—often ill-fitting mysteries—to write so as to produce something hardly understood by himself and not at all by others, not remembering that clarity, ease, and directness of thought are the glory of good poets' writings. Whereas the good poets are delightful and profitable to those who devote themselves to reading them, the others remain so odious that it could be said they do not write for others but for themselves.* Great prudence, therefore, should be exercised by those who would blend the philosophic with the poetic.

The rule can be this: Whenever the philosophic is obscure or does not carry with it poetic glory and grace to lift up the reader's or hearer's mind, then the writer ought to refrain from showing himself a philosopher and to come forth a beautiful and gentle poet, rather than, in an attempt to blend the divine, the natural, and the moral, to become sluggish, arid, harsh, unpleasing, distorted, obscure, and tedious; thus it is always necessary to have an interpreter at hand to untie the knots and to throw light on its darkness, to the reader's or hearer's disgust, and with censure of the writer. Although this kind of writing sometimes accompanies satire (I am not speaking of the dramatic), it is not decorous for the heroic, the elegiac, or the lyric poet, though it is almost a characteristic of the lyric to be somewhat difficult.

He should also know that all the things the poet chooses to say (whether gathered from the gardens of poesy or the fields of philosophy) should be written and said with even style, so that the writer or speaker may not at one time go up, and another time go down, and the verses appear to be at strife. This is indeed a great fault and much annoying to the judicious hearer or reader. Since I have said enough about this above, I shall not speak further of it now.

Imitation The completion of this part should include a discussion of imitation. I do not speak of that which is imitative of human actions, by which the writer is called a poet, nor of that pertaining to the invention and the arrangement, which has been discussed in various places in our treatise, but of that imitation which in the expression of the senses is with the grace and splendor of words—that which entirely concerns elocution and its phases. This imitation (as it seems to me) is no other than a diligent and judicious consideration that we may use, by means of like observation, to become excellent in expression and to practice it thoroughly in order to reach the mark that it reached. This imitation resides in the model to whose image we strive to make our style conform. This is done by exercise and by reading those whom we would imitate and by composing continuously in the likeness of such works. But since we discussed this matter sufficiently in our other works, both Latin and vulgar, I shall not now go on much further about it, referring anyone who wants to know of such matters in this language to my *Poetics*.

Indeed as far as the present treatise is concerned, I say

that some have thought imitation to be only a certain air (as the painters and singers are accustomed to say of their art) given to the writings which makes them similar to that from which they are derived. These persons maintain that this air comes only from a particular judgment that causes one to note certain things in the writer whom he is following as model (as the painter in his art notes colors and lineaments), which make him bear a likeness to that writer whom he imitates. Though perhaps this view does not deserve complete refutation, yet since, so stated, it rather confuses, I shall leave it to whoever deems he may expound it better. I shall say now that the imitator should avoid being so intent on the choice of words drawn from him whom he imitates that he is satisfied only with these. Although this may be quite necessary in imitation, it is not the only thing that ought to give pause to him who wishes to make himself like his model for the rule of writing. He ought also to consider the order, the terms, the joining of the words, and the positions in which, as in their own place, the one he chose to imitate lodged these words in expressing his thoughts. This point does not pertain so much to disposition as to elocution, one of the branches of invention, for, in trying to write elegantly, one should know how important is the placing of any word for both the grace and cogency of the discourse. One ought to be no less diligent in considering the figures of speech, the length and shortness of the rhythmical cadences, what are the perfect terms, what are the parts of the terms, and with what jointures and orders this and that are placed to form the body of the composition designed by the author he is imitating. From these things come the order, the harmony, and the rhythm; so important are these that, if they are neglected by the imitator, or imitated unattentively—even if he should possess all the other virtues of the author he has chosen as model—he would never be able to be like him.

Today those who imitate Boccaccio fall into this error; concentrating on the choice of the words he used, they are content to place them in fine company. Since they have all other things and the other major excellencies, I do not know if I ought to speak in disgust or [say] that, because of their little realized ignorance, they consider themselves brothers to Boccaccio for having sometimes mingled his words in their compositions. If then anyone with judgment reads such, he finds such unlikeness between them and Boccaccio that it seems they tried to make themselves like anyone else but him. Among these heedless imitators are some of such twisted judgment as to think that changing the order of the discourse, not only in words but in members, is the way to be like him whom they imitate. This is far removed from good imitation, since changing the order and the measure is nothing other than reversing the members and making them disproportionate and therefore lame, as if the writings were to walk with one leg long and the other short, or with feet up and head down. In this way the composition comes out, as an imitation, a monster rather than something based on the model from which the imitation was drawn. And so they show that they have toiled to their shame and have revealed their lack of judgment. If beauty is nothing other than a fitting, ordered, and measured proportion of the members, strewn with delightful colors, and this beauty is desirable in discourse as in other things that have grandeur, how can beauty be assimilated in such disproportion from the model from which the writers would derive their imitation? Furthermore, if the grave and the acute of the words is what makes the sound, and the long and the short is what gives the measure of the time, i.e., the rhythm, how can the rhythm and the sound function if the words are reversed, and, put in other positions, produce another rhythm and sound? That variation in these two things, in altering the order, so modifies the discourse that the second has no similarity to the first (I speak with respect to elocution) even if perhaps similar to its thought. Although in prose writings this thing is seen clearly by good judges, it is not discerned in verse. When the order of words in verse is changed, so changed is the quantity of the syllables that it is no longer verse; if it does remain verse (this rarely happens), it is of another meter and sound than it was before.

Needless to say here, this would not be other than insisting that the same clauses and compositions be used; this should be discarded as foolish, since there can be the same order, the same rhythm, and the same sound in a variety of words which make a discourse different from the original, as regards words, but quite similar in sound and rhythm.

If this is easy for the poet, it ought to be easier for the orator, who is not as strictly bound by metrical rhythm. If one should tell me that Boccaccio himself often said the same thing with words, rhythm, and sounds other than the original words he used, and that another rhythm and sound was created, I should say that he speaks the truth. In this respect he did in his language what Cicero did when he attempted to imitate Roscius, to see if he could vary similar meanings just as Roscius expressed himself differently with various gestures.[164] Our Boccaccio did not intend to imitate such variation, but rather to set out for us, by the bounty of his divine genius and the rare eloquence that reigned in him, varied manners of language expressing the same thought. One of these was not precisely like the other, though all of them carried the same thought. This is not dissimilar to a father who, after his first child, begets other children; though they come from him, he is not disturbed that all are not identical with the first; and so, though all are begotten by him and have some semblance to their father and therefore are not at all dissimilar, one is not another. He who will try to paint Horace will not paint Curtius or Sergius (if these children may be so named). This variation, then, found in Boccaccio in expressing the same thing differently is not for imitation but to show that our language is not so poor as not to be able to say the same thing well in many ways. If each imitator will strive to imitate in the same way, he will win my approval. But if in the light of this model of Boccaccio's variation, he should mix up the members in the way we described, I shall never call him an imitator but rather a bungler of beautiful and pleasing discourse. In my opinion, rather than fall into this vice, it is better if the writer chooses Boccaccio's words in a manner of language fitting to himself than with this confusion to attempt to be like Boccaccio. When the writer so intends, he will achieve this similitude, if in changing words judiciously he makes the sound and the rhythm fit the members, as we said.

An admirable imitator of Cicero (I shall not hesitate to cite a Latin model, even though I am discussing things in the vulgar) was Lactantius Firmianus.[165] If he had been as close an observer of the words as of the rhythm, I would venture to say that he came closer to Cicero than any other writer, including those in our time. But the matter to which he set his hand was perhaps the reason his discourse was not of that purity requisite for imitation. Others of our time (except two or three) have followed every other thing except the rhythm and the sound. Some have approached his ease of style and have remained childishly immature; others, his seriousness and remained obscure; still others, his sentences and remained little less than parched dry. Some have imitated only the beauty and remained empty, others undertook his happiest spaciousness and remained like boatmen lost on a vast ocean. There are also those who are given to twisting, breaking, changing, shortening, lengthening the members and remain so confused that trying to be virtuous they fall into vice.

Imitation, then, ought to be proportionate to the model the imitator set for himself and to fit not just one or two members but all the parts in such a way that, seeking to assimilate one part, he does not neglect another, but considers them all equally and then carries them over into his composition so that they become his own and so that his composition is no longer like the composition of the model he took for his guide; so that it is the son of the father, the brother of the other, come into life from the same source as the other; and however much alike, are so unlike that the one is clearly not the other.

Since the words are found for the sentences (i.e., for the thoughts, which Aristotle called sentences), those will have well imitated who, after choosing the words and the ordered arrangement of them, will so accompany the sentences with these words that the sound and the rhythm will be as a mate to the grace, majesty, strength, splendor, and liveliness of that which the imitator sought to assimilate. More than all others Monsignor Bembo did this admirably in the poems he composed in imitation of Petrarch, especially in the double sestina of his *Asolani*[166] made like that of Petrarch on the death of Laura.[167] In this Bembo succeeded so well that it could occupy first place if Petrarch's had not been born first. He did the same in those Latin letters that are called *Brevi* (insofar as he could grasp the usage and the quality of the bishops' writing), composed in imitation of Cicero. Although these often have the same theme and form of speaking, this happy genius varied them so thoroughly that, by his prudence and the other virtues infused in them, the judicious read them more willingly than those of many others who have had a large field to find varied subjects and have wasted themselves in empty and futile nonsense. If these have more adherents than Bembo and those like him, it is because they are more corrupt than sane judges who choose as example that which is agreeable to them. Like the example [of Bembo], this same will happen in the imitation of all who will recognize what is good; by practicing reading and writing, using good authors as models, they will create so as to transmute imitation into nature (this should be foremost in the imitator's mind) in such a way that it will be impossible not to write like him to whose imitation they will have turned the virtue and force of their talent. Finally enabled to perform, they will act like little birds which, leaving the nest and having flown for awhile—after having learned from their father and mother how to fly—feel themselves firm on their wings, then spread them boldly through the air with no aid and direct their flight bravely wherever they please.

To achieve this goal, it is helpful to know how to recognize what makes the author to be imitated merit such praise that others deem him worthy to be chosen as model and, having recognized this, to know how to put it into practice. Imitation should always be accompanied by emulation, which is simply a firm desire to surpass him whom one imitates. This desire motivates one not to be content to equal him whom he follows, but to strive so to excel that he may become first and merit being imitated by others instead of the one he first imitated.† Nor is this as difficult as one may think, if the imitator is resolute and focuses all his forces into achieving this goal. It is easy for a runner, after reaching the point he set before him, to pass it and leave it behind. In these days mother nature has not become such an unloving stepmother to men in eloquence and now so poor that she does not give them power to excel in imitable things those who are regarded as preeminent. The divine Vergil did so in imitating Homer; it seemed that he set before him that great Greek, most excellent master of the heroic poem among the Greeks up to Vergil's time, not only to make himself like him but to excel him so that he was first, Homer second. The Right Reverend Sadoletto[168] aimed at this when he composed his *Laocoon*. As Vergil had surpassed Homer, so he in turn thought to surpass Vergil. Whether or not he achieved this I would have others judge. I shall venture to say that he showed us clearly that men of good talents are not so terrified by the excellencies of great poets as not to think of equaling and surpassing them. Even if often they try in vain, their desire is nonetheless laudable.

Petrarch left far behind him all the old Tuscans who wrote before him, and our Ariosto so stood apart from the others in the quality of his works that he alone among them (speaking universally) was found worthy of imitation. All this comes from judgment, valid in this respect as in all others. But I think I have gone on further about this

Vitality of a Poem

than I proposed. So ending here this discussion, I shall begin talking about that aspect of composition concerned with giving life to the work and how, shall we say, it is apprehended in the mind. I am not here considering this matter in the manner of Aristotle when he said that the plot is the soul of the work. There he does not take *anima* (mind, soul) in the sense of vitality as, following the view of Plutarch, I now take it. He used *anima* in that context as *subject*, without which the existence of the work would be taken away; indeed, it holds the same place in the poem as the vegetable soul (which Monsignor Sadoletto called the *anima* of life in his philosophy) holds with respect to the other souls *(anime)* or of the other qualities of the soul in the body. For just as if the vegetable soul were taken from man, all the other souls or powers would be lacking, so if the plot *(favola)* were taken away, everything else about the poem would be lacking; as was stated above, everything else is considered in relation to the plot.

Now, turning to the subject: One is to know that what we call the soul, with respect to orators, is manifested in the utterance and actions (everything pertaining not only to words but to the grace and dignity of the movements of the head, face, eyes, hands, and all the body while the orator speaks) and is intended to give spirit and life to the whole oration; it was called by the father of the Latin language the eloquence of the body. Although this same thing is also in the poet, especially that kind of poetry which, as we said, received the name of canto for its parts from the recitation in the presence of great masters; nevertheless, it seems to me that the soul of the poem is to be found in respects other than utterance; namely, in the force and virtue of the writing, whence the emotions enter the heart of the reader as if it were a living voice speaking, so that not only when the poem is recited (if perchance the poet ever does so) but when it is read by another, it seems a living body.

It also seems to me that the words can be so significant and so apt in revealing the thoughts as to be impressed on the reader's mind with such efficacy and vehemence that one feels their force and is moved to participate in the emotions under the veil of words in the poet's verses. This is the *Enargeia*, which does not reside in the minute (as we said above that Trissino believed) but in putting the thing clearly and effectively before the reader's eyes and in the hearer's ears, assuming that this is done artfully with appropriate words (to which the ancients gave dignity for their own quality) which are, as it were, born together with the thing. Of greatest force are borrowed words, which Aristotle called strange or foreign;[169] likewise comparisons, similitudes, adjuncts (called by the Greeks epithets, by the Latins adjectives). Among the other figures of speech the hyperbole and also newly coined words were often used effectively to the end we are now discussing. All these matters belong to elocution and were taken by the writers of rhetoric for its ornament; however, since we are now considering words not only in relation to embellishment and grace but also more in relation to force and vivacity than to the former, we prefer to speak now particularly of the latter. The former are only for ornament and beauty, and the latter, besides the ornament they have in themselves, are effective, as Plutarch says, for efficacy, spirit, and soul in what we write.

Aristotle named current native words ornate because the Hellenic words on the whole are the most beautiful and most fit that can be discovered, to put so charmingly and vividly before the reader's eyes the matter to be expressed that it appears to be viewed as done. But these words can be drawn from the common usage of the people's speech and from observation of excellent and approved writers. Words from common usage are easier and make the discourse clearer and faster, but common usage is often too low and too degraded. From observation are derived the significant, magnificent, serious, sonorous words of such splendor that they fill the discourse with light. These are more for the poet, except that it might seem to him better on occasion, for the greater expression of some emotion, to choose from popular words, as did Petrarch when he said: "Che vergogna con man da gli occhi forba." Here the word *forba* (first used by Dante, who put into his *Comedy* more plebeian words than were necessary for careful writing), in itself vile and low, conforms to the naturally vulgar act and puts this effect superbly before the reader's eyes, sometimes so much is the similarity of nature to art, and so much the efficacy and force of vulgar words to propriety.‡

Metaphors Transferred or metaphorical words were those that, in the beginnings of languages, were found because of inadequacy of that language; the translators, lacking the proper words, used the translated; that is, those which had some likeness to the matter they had to express. Then after languages were enriched, and it was seen how much force, splendor, and light they carried in them in the greater abundance of words, they were accepted for poetic as well as for oratorical discourse.§ Hence they are sometimes used rather than the proper and the natural. The transferred or metaphorical word is similar in meaning to the one it replaces, to signify this or that, as calling the sails the wings of a ship, their oars, the wings of angels; and as saying sleepy for careless, the celestial fires for the stars (one writer who made a heroic poem far from the acceptable form in our language called them the heads of heaven's nails),¶ and other kinds of speech used for better expression to hide ugliness, to increase or to decrease the subject matter, and for its embellishment.

In these transfers, called metaphors by the Greeks, the writer ought to be very prudent to find and use them with much selection, since they are not to be put haphazardly into the work; and because of their inequality with those whose place they take, they annoy the reader or even cause him to laugh, as the one we cited about the stars, called by the aforesaid writer the heads of heaven's nails. One should also be careful about choosing metaphors that consist not of a single word like those cited above but of words dragged out at length. These should always be in similitude and sustained to the end, not done as one who, praising Monsignor Bembo, began his sonnet with flying and ended it with weaving. I see this fault so often in many writers that I do not know how they can be so blind as not to see the error plainly. I think this comes about because they do not practice logic, which, as it befuddles the brain of one who does not understand it, so it makes lucid and clear the discourse of one who is intelligently acquainted with it and its modes. Logic will never let one who comes out of its school well instructed fall into these stupidities. By following the way Petrarch expresses metaphors, they can see how others ought to be used. In the sonnet beginning "Passa la nave mia colma di oblio,"[170] having set out to compare his travails in love to a ship battered by a storm, he sustains this figure to the end. The same is seen in the sonnet "S'amore, o morte non da qualche stroppio";[171] here, having begun the similitude with the figure of weaving, he ends it in weaving, not in flying or sailing.

I do not say this because in any one sonnet there cannot be more than one metaphor, as is seen in the sonnet "Gia disiai con si giusta querela,"[172] but because the composer was alert not to put forward one similitude and then, speaking like one possessed or indeed of an insane mind, his memory lost and beside himself, to pass unmindfully from one to another. No less, in relation to this, should affectation be avoided; if prominent in a work it is always injurious and very unseemly, more than any other fault we have discussed; indeed, in metaphorical language it is wholly disgusting. I recall having heard a preaching friar who, having worked up to a heat in reprehending lechery, said, to attract attention, here the foot of the intellect stops in the field of the mind. He took up much time with this and other inane metaphors which were so annoying to those of good taste that they regretted being there; but, since they were and could not leave gracefully, they were sorry they were not deaf and could not hear them.

Of great worth will be those metaphors that are not far from common speech, because our minds receive gladly what is recognizable. Nevertheless one ought to be careful not to deal too much in the popular because such is of little force; likewise, the tragic and the too grand should be avoided because they show too much affectation; and also those drawn out too long—as if we should say, he used on me the dagger of anger and did me in with sharp words cutting bloody wounds—because these are far from commonsense. The obscure are also of little worth because, when they ought to give light to the discourse, they really bring shadows and dimness. Above all others that do not fit are those like the monsters we spoke of and gave examples of above. Let us now proceed without saying anything further about this matter, referring to what I have already written about it to that happy spirit Giulio Pontio,[173] my dear disciple, whom, in the finest flowering of his age and promise, importunate death robbed, to the great sorrow of talented men and to the inestimable loss of the better studies.

Concerning these metaphors it should be noted that although the similitude was the foundation and origin of the metaphor, the metaphor is always different from the similitude in that the latter is a comparison with the things we wish to express, as one could say, man is a creature as is the bird. The metaphor stands for the thing itself, as can be seen in the examples of the wings and the sails cited above; and as Petrarch did when he said: "Pioggia di lagrimar, nebbia di sdegno,"[174] where rain *(pioggia)* stands for tears and fog *(nebbia)* for perturbation of the mind and face. Petrarch also used the metaphor artistically in many places, but especially in the sonnet "Gia disiai con si giusta querela."[175] Of this we said above that it bears in itself such splendor that more could not be desired in delineating with varied metaphors the subject of love in this language.

A sure rule about metaphors cannot be given, because, as Aristotle said, they cannot be taught and therefore they cause the utmost difficulty, making necessary continual use, observation, and practice in composition.**

New Words I call as new words those not in the usage of common speech and writing which are put into poems for greater expression of what is written, as Petrarch did in the *Triumph of Time* when he said: "Quattro cavai con quanto studio como,"[176] where he used *comare*, a word not in common writing and speech, perhaps intending to say what he expressed with the verb without using a baser or less significant word. Besides, the introduction of this word allowed him to make a fitting and significant rhyme. Monsignor Bembo, a most observant writer, used *venerata*, a word no longer used, which I know from old esteemed authors in this language, though he had available the word *honorata*, which he could have well used; nevertheless, he regarded the former one as more fitting to convey his thought, which, in this stanza, required a word meaning not only honor but also devoted reverence for the divine. Therefore he said: "Tanto ci son temuta, & venerata."[177] In the first and second editions he had the line "Tanto vi son temuta, & vencrata"; then, in the third, he judiciously changed *vi* to *ci*. Ariosto also used (to give only one example of the many words he introduced felicitously) *esterrefatta* (terror) when he could have said *impaurita* (terror), in "L'esterrefatta subito famiglia." Because it seemed to him that the former word would put before the eyes of the reader this sudden terror more expressively than the latter, he used the former and omitted the latter. Though these words should be used only rarely, they create a remarkable effect when the judicious writer puts them prudently into compositions at the right time and place, but he ought to be very cautious about using these new words lest he fall into the vice of Sesena in the

Roman times, who thought that to speak contrary to the usage of good orators was to speak well, as Cicero said where he mentions him in the book of excellent orators.[178]

Comparisons give the breath of life and great merit to poetry. In his *Partitions*, Cicero, it seems, would have them be about the quantity of things, i.e., from more to less, or from less to more, or equal.[179] From the more to the less, the comparison is made in this manner: The dearer certain things are, the less esteemed the doubtful; from less to more: The less one strives for gold and gems, the more he will strive for glory and honor; on equal things: Aeneas was as much praised by Vergil as Achilles was by Homer. Some maintain that this third kind of comparison is the same as similitude, others that it is not, that there is much difference. But leaving now this question to those who are devoted to studying these things more diligently, I say that the poet does not make the similitude as to quantity but quality, as if he should say: The fury of the people is like the wrath of the sea when it rages. However, it should be noted that our poets have made little or no distinction between the similitude and the comparison and have indeed taken the one for the other, as (commonly interpreted) did the Greek and Latin poets, so that it seems this minute difference pertains more to the orator than to the poet. Be that as it may, comparisons are of great worth and incomparable liveliness for a work, when they are not too low, or too obscure, or drawn out too long.

But before I go further, I should warn the poet that in narrations, ostentatiously long comparisons are not fitting. This is bad practice, since narration ought to be pure, lucid,

Comparisons

easy, and without affectation; only those comparisons are suitable to it which are brief and which would actually be used in common discourse. This should especially be noted: For a person at the time of deep pain to discourse ostentatiously is untimely and contrary to decorum, particularly when the speaker is ill or near death. Therefore there are those who censure Ariosto, who in the twenty-first canto has Hermonide, mortally wounded by Zerbino, telling of the misfortune of Gabrina in high-sounding comparisons. It seems to them that a person afflicted as he was ought not to indulge in such ostentatious language.

It is no less true that if the narration is so long drawn out that it takes up a great number of verses and is introduced into the poem as an episode, the comparisons are just as fitting there as they are in the rest of the work, provided that such is narrated by a person at leisure who is not involved in grief immediately pressing on him. An example of this is in the second and third books of Vergil's *Aeneid*; however, Homer in the ninth book of the *Odyssey* refrained from comparisons when he introduced Ulysses telling of his wanderings, and depended on long descriptions rather than high-sounding comparisons. I believe this came about because few comparisons are used in the whole *Odyssey*, whereas there are many in the *Iliad*, since the latter is grander and more sublime, the former much humbler as compared with the *Iliad*. Although the first six books of Vergil resemble (as we said) the twenty-four of the *Odyssey*, nevertheless, in them he put more comparisons than Homer used. The reason was that, since he composed the whole *Aeneid*[††] in the grand and magnificent mode and took from Homer only what was suitable to the majesty of his work, he was focusing upon the glorious action of a single hero. Therefore, having reduced to twelve books (insofar as fitted his imitation) what Homer had written in forty-eight books of the actions of two heroes, it was fitting that each part of his work conform to that illustrious action which he had chosen to imitate; here one part could not be humble, another dignified, since both parts were structured into a single action.

The adjuncts, which are the epithets of things or of the words called substantives, are like lights giving luminous vivacity to the composition.‡‡ Although these have, as has the metaphor, something of strangeness, yet they are very different; the metaphor is put in place of its own word, whereas the epithets are accompanied by their own words, by means of their closeness to the very name of the things. Their use is more suited to the poet than to the orator, who ought to use them more temperately and circumspectly than the poet, since simplicity of speech is more fitting to the orator than to the poet. His fictions, if not adorned with fitting flowers and pleasing ornaments, remain inept; whence it is, if the poet uses some word that is not necessary but ornaments the work so that the word is not superfluous, it is accepted by good judges. But without such epithets as, for instance, white snow, soft wax, cold frost, light feather, the nature of the thing is known and understood; for as soon as one says *snow* we know that it is white, and we know wax is of itself soft; frost is cold, and a feather is light without any additional words. It may be seen therefore that what gives spirit and life to the poet, with respect to composition, would on the whole be superfluous to the orator.

Adjuncts or Epithets

The adjuncts ought not to be too long or too frequent

or untimely; those too long show fastidiousness, those too frequent, affectation; they make the oration (as Aristotle said of Alcidamas[180]) cold and frosty, and it appears to the reader's eyes not alive but rotten and decayed. Those used untimely and out of keeping with the nature of the thing to which they are joined are inept; these appear superfluous and unnecessary and are put into compositions only to fill them out. Many of our poets today can be charged with this vice. Intent only on bringing a verse to its end, they do not consider with what art and grace they handle them. What could be finished in two verses they spread out into a whole stanza, with useless and insignificant words, securing with trouble the consonance of the rhyme because of this languidness. Granted that the attempt to give consonance to the rhyme was often the reason for prolonging the sentence, by circumlocution or by metaphor or by parentheses or by comparisons or by similar means necessary for the composer to use, nevertheless he ought to take great pains not to run into languidness so that the ornament becomes paltriness or seems a scrap of cloth patched on to fill out the number of the verses.

As adjuncts were introduced into compositions by the better judges in order that their speech or writing might not be like the vulgar, so if these are used at the wrong time and unfitly, they make more than plebeian the elocution and compositions of whoever uses them. And so in other matters as in this, the author ought always to have a certain measure so that he may not allow himself to go over into excessiveness.§§ Sannazaro slipped into this error in his *Arcadia* and Boccaccio in his *Ameto*. Likewise (in the opinion of some) Tibullus among the Latins slipped into it; for this reason some had rather imitate Propertius than Tibullus. But this abundance of epithets is eminently suited to the elegy (say who will to the contrary), which does not deal with anything serious but is all about the soft and delicate, and about rhetorical flowers and the delights of poetry. Knowing this, the judicious Navagero[181] and good Molza[182] modeled themselves upon Tibullus in their elegiac verses rather than upon any other Latin poet who wrote verses dealing with such matter. But, although Aristotle thought that epithets ought to have similitude with the thing to which they are joined and that paltriness results if they are not so used,[183] nonetheless, the usage of our language is fond of epithets contrary to the nature of the things to which they are joined, as *dannoso guadagno* (injurious gain), *util danno* (profitable loss), *pigra velocita* (lazy speed), *ordine confuso* (confused order), *trista allegrezza* (sorrowful gaiety), *gelato foco* (chill fire), *infiammata neve* (inflamed snow),¶ and others like them, almost infinite. In the use of these Petrarch was most eminent not only in the *Canzoniere* but also in the *Triumphs*; also Monsignor Bembo in his poem in terza rima addressed to the ladies.[184] It is true that this kind is more suited to the amorous than to the dignified mode; yet when these adjuncts are put skillfully into the dignified, they lend great force and remarkable worth to the discourse, as is seen in this verse of Petrarch: "Nel cor pien d'amarissima dolcezza." And when speaking of Laura's mind in the *Triumph of Death*, he wrote: "Morte bella parea nel suo bel viso."[185]

Although the word *bella* accompanied by *morte* does not carry in itself a manifest contradiction, as does *amarissima* with *dolcezza*, it is indeed contrary to the nature of the thing to which it is joined, since nothing is more obscure to men nor more hateful nor more repellant than death (speaking now of the common thought of men and leaving out the saying that philosophy is nothing other than the contemplation of death and the knowledge that it is beautiful), nevertheless speaking of it in the face of the dead lady as beautiful shows most effectively her beauty when she lived.

Sometimes adverbs also create the effect of adjuncts, as is seen in Petrarch when he said: "Dodici donne honestamente lasse,"[186] where the adverb *honestamente* shows very artfully the sweet and chaste activity of these ladies. In Ariosto also is a most effective expression of love when he said: "Affettuosamente inamorato." And in our *Orbecche*, to show an increased speed, we also wrote to this effect: "Velocissimamente caminare."

I shall not now go on to show whether epithets or adjuncts are tropes or figures, as do those who put more figures in writing than there are words, since with such futile diligence (perhaps useless in our language), I do not now wish to be wearied but to leave such matters to those who would rather exercise the function of schoolmasters than be critics of the force and life of writing. It suffices me to have pointed out the value of such modes of discoursing and how much spirit and life they may give to a discourse if they are used with the prudence that ought always to guide writers.

Hyperbole The hyperbole (which we would classify as a figure of speech that is beyond belief and that we employ to make larger or to lessen what we are speaking of) sometimes gives a certain effectiveness to verse and to the meaning, especially if it is used in the manner of a comparison or a similitude, as we would like to call it, as in Petrarch when he said of the burning of amorous fire:

> Non bolle mai Vulcan, Lipari, od Ischia,
> Stromboli, o Mongibel con tanta rabbia:
> Misero e ben, chi in tal gioco s'arrischia.[187]

This hyperbole shows most effectively the mode of the thought, as also the one that Ercole Strozza used (though in another form) in the tercets of one of his sonnets. I shall not be burdensome if I put it down in this discussion, because it seems to me worthy of your reading, also because it was not ascribed by the printers to another author as was this other one by Strozza which begins:

> Euro gentil, che gli avrei crespi nodi
> Hor quinci, hor quindi pel bel volto giri.[188]

This they published under the name of Baldassare Castiglione, a gentleman in himself so famous and illustrious, both in actions and in his compositions, that he had no need of the words of another for his own fame and reputation. This is the sonnet:

> Triomphal, gloriosa, & lieta barca
>   Che si bella Sirena pel mar porti,
>   Quanti sian per te presi? & quanti morti?
>   D'amorosi Trophei ti veggio ir carca.
> Via piu saggio d'Vlisse e, chi ti varca,
>   Sordo al suon, cieco a i guardi vaghi e accorti.
>   Deh perche non bramai prima i di corti,
>   Che senza te in filar stancar la Parca?
> Miro i pesci adunarsi, & d'ogni intorno
>   Volar gli augelli, & stare i venti, & l'acque
>   Al suave concento, al viso adorno.
> La Sirena del ciel subito tacque;
>   Fermossi il polo, & raddoppiossi il giorno;
>   Tanto udirla, & vederla a ciascun piacque.[189]

    Petrarch used this figure quite artistically although without comparison, when he said:

> Avrei fatto parlando,
> Romper le pietre, & pianger di dolcezza.[190]

Elsewhere he said: "Che farian gire i monti, & stare i fiumi."[191] These examples are enough, I think, to show the force of this figure.***

The Sententia Next the sentence (sententia), which gets its ornaments from apothegms (which are certain acute and brief sayings of great and learned men), from proverbs (which are common sayings that fall from the lips of men almost like usage in common speech), and from diverse others called figures of things by the Greeks and Latins. The knowledge of illustrious things gives to the sentences great strength as the variety gives suavity to them, freshness and grandeur of things which they carry within them, with the efficacious brevity by which they include a great thought in very few words. The sentences are more effective in discourse than the other parts in that they are not under the shadow of the words but close to the things expressed with naked words; and the authority of the things is much greater than that of the words.

Naked Words I call naked words those that do not have with them any ornaments except their own property in themselves. Although the force of the sentence is great in every kind of discourse, it is greatest in verse, since, carried by the smoothness of the metrical rhythm to everyone's ears, it enters the mind, like a dart hurled by a strong arm, deeply piercing it with remarkable pleasure and imprints within it what it speaks of. The sentence therefore is not other (as far as it pertains to our present purpose) than a form of speech in accord with custom, drawn from common life and thought of men, which shows effectively with pleasing brevity either what has been or what is or what ought to be in human life. These are frequent in tragedy, as superlatively fitting to put the action, the emotions, the customs, the terrible, the pitiable before the spectators' eyes. And as facetiousness, witticism, and salty pungency in comedies incite laughter, so in tragedies the sentences generate seriousness and wonder when they come into the work not falsely nor outside the nature of the thing, but naturally as though born with it. When they seem false (as do many in the tragedies of our time), they are only tedious to the reader or hearer, as are facetiousness, witticism, and salty pungency used out of time and place in comedies. Plautus committed this fault so often that it seems he put first the inciting of laughter as the aim of his comedies, as if he wrote not comedies but mimes, in which it is fitting to move laughter by means of manifest ugliness and unseemly nonsense. In this particular matter Bibiena also yielded (although he showed high genius) in his *Calandria*, having followed Plautus, who for this fault was censured deservedly by Horace.[192]

To return to the primary topic, it seems too strange to the hearer or reader for the writer to leave his proper subject to make one laugh or to go seeking an outlandish thought or one scarcely congruous with what he is writing about. Trissino frequently slipped into this vice in his *Italia*, as a judicious reader of it can clearly see. He was much more careful in this respect in his *Sophonisba*, which doubtless holds first place in his writings and is highly praiseworthy, although in many places of it he was more given to write of the customs and manners of the Greeks than was fitting for a Roman work portraying majesty of persons as he did in *Sophonisba*. But since I discussed this matter at length in the discourse I addressed to Pontio,[193] it suffices now to have touched on it lightly.

To pursue the topic of sentences: Some of them are called simple not in the manner stated by Hermogenes in the second book of his forms where he treats of simplicity,[194] but in that they convey a single thought, as, for example, everyone has his fortune from the day he was born; people to whom night comes before evening; he dies well who dying escapes pain; a beautiful death wholly honors life. Some sentences are used instead of logical argument, which they include in themselves and are taken for such; they therefore are more extensive in words than others, like this one I now imagine for you: Since the more deceiving fortune is, the more she seems favorable to a man; therefore, he who enjoys her favors ought to be much afraid and he who finds her adverse ought to have good hope. Other sentences are neither simple nor logical but partake of both; these are most charming and worth much in giving spirit to the work, as if it were said: A thing divine does not belong to a mortal. Here the words *mortal* and *divine* have in themselves the logic of the sentence, not expressed but hinted at artfully.

Next are those called twofold or ambiguous, because they are made up of diverse or contrary elements. Those of contrary are like these: Good fortune makes a man insolent; trouble subdues him to modesty. Those of diverse elements are like this one: Virtue pleases more than any other thing, but labor whence it is acquired displeases. Sentences are also made by similitude or by comparison, as if I were to say: Weeping increases sorrow as the rain fills the streams. There are also those by similitude or by comparison and contrast, as: Unchaste pleasure causes more harm to one's mind than great sorrow. Some sentences are uttered with interrogation; some by comparison, as we said before; others are adapted to things, others to persons. Of this variety I shall not take the trouble now to set out further examples, since the larger part of this matter pertains to the orator rather than to the poet; and in writing to you, Messer Giovambattista, it suffices that I only mention these things.

I shall not fail to tell you, however, that the subjects of the sentences pertain to manners and human life. The poet will find the sentences artistically fitting if he will stay close to what pertains to the customs, to the common thought of men, and to events that occur most frequently, always restricting speech to the universal and common, not to particular persons, because, as soon as sentences are reduced to the particular, they lose the name and fall short of being sentences. If one should say, virtue shines brighter than any treasure, it would be a sentence, since it is common and universal or indeed is uttered indeterminately; but if one should say, virtue shines brighter than the treasure of Argos, it would cease immediately to be a sentence. Therefore Plutarch defined the sentence as a universal statement that pertains to human life and affairs.[195] I am not unaware that there are ancient authors who think the contrary, but in my opinion they are mistaken about this.

Granted that sentences by their nature tend to be brief; nevertheless, the poet (as does the orator) sometimes works to make the sentence yield a logical statement in itself and to extend its length. If this is done in a pleasing manner, it proves a very happy way of giving spirit to the composition, as can be seen in this stanza:

> Chi beneficio ad altrui face, deve
> Usar gran diligenza in ben locarlo:
> Che spesso cerca con angoscia greve
> Ingrato cor del ben ricompensarlo,
> Et tutto quel, ch'ad huom benigno deve,
> Nella parte peggior cerca di trarlo;
> Che non si muta il reo per beneficio,
> Ne cura l'ingrat'huom cortesse ufficio.[196]

Besides the foregoing matters, we are also to consider at this point that, as splendor of words is necessary in leisurely parts, so it is damaging in the sentences, since the dazzling light of the words blinds that of the sentence; it should therefore be put into the poem with significant but naked words, without imposing ornamentation. Nor should the poet link together so many sentences in his composition that the course of the statement may be interrupted oftener than necessary and thereby become hard and lacking in smoothness. As the distribution of them throughout the composition in appropriate places lends so much splendor and force that it aids in giving soul and spirit, so slowness and languidness result when they are introduced too frequently. For their frequency makes them appear like unbound brooms, as can be illustrated in the prose works of the Latins in Seneca's *Moralia* and in Petrarch in his little book *De remediis utriusque fortunae;* and in the Greek by Plutarch's *Moralia*, in which he so admirably imitated Seneca that he set out not only the virtues but also the vices in treating the same topics many times.

To conclude and sum up this part pertaining to the life and spirit: One should know that the rule of all the parts of the poem is measure. Indeed it is to be known that one who always falls short in decorum of words in metaphors *(trallationi)*, in innovations of words, in adjuncts, in hyperbole, in sentences, and in other pertinent aspects, not only will not make the work live but will kill it and bury it in a dark tomb. There are as many things that give vital liveliness to a discourse as there are that detract from it, since those same ornaments badly used take away life from it, leaving it crude and causing it to die. It happens to them as we see it happening in the humors of human bodies; as humors are the cause of good health when they are in their natural and balanced conditions, so they are the cause of infirmity and death when they depart from their equitable nature.

In embellishing his poem, therefore, the poet ought to do as the painter does with figures; as the latter, with varieties of colors and shades blended and distributed artfully, makes the figure beautiful and pleasing to the beholder's eyes, so the poet, with variety of ornaments and the placing of other parts that are not ornaments, ought to give grace, life, and spirit to his poem. Poetry is like a picture[197] that has life and speech. If one is to err in one of the two ways of erring, it is better to submit to the too-little (if I shall not weary you by reiterating this most profitable principle) than to the too-much, for if those things which greatly please and delight the senses and convey in themselves in the first impression the greatest force are seen at first too often or in too great abundance, they give us not pleasure but incredible irritation. Whence it can be seen that, as irritation lies close at hand to unmeasured pleasure, so excessive reiteration of these excellencies of the work causes, if not death, at least annoyance and satiety so great that one cannot possess the patience to read them. This

Poetry and Painting

indeed happens to those who profess to be erudite, who load everything they compose with proverbs, exempla, fables, stories, jokes, customs, philosophies, and old, difficult, foreign words, so that they make their discourse like the driest sand. If they had put in such things with moderation and order, they would have enhanced and embellished the work marvelously. These indeed fall into this vice, but so also do many of those in our time professing Greek who make no oration or preamble or letter which they do not try to make two-thirds Greek—a vice that so much offended Cicero (although he was not less versed in the Greek language than in the Latin) that in his orations and preambles he never used ten Greek words in succession except when he adduced some authority, as he did with the verses of Hesiod where he treats of virtue.[198] In no other composition is there an example of this idiom; and he never put any into his familiar letters except those necessary to what he discussed. But ostentation blinds some in our day and causes them to incur censure where they think to win praise, exposing their distorted and corrupted judgment in composition.†††

Achieving Enargeia The things we have stated, therefore, along with others which as lesser matters come behind them or are drawn from them (it did not seem fitting or necessary to put into this little book of ours all that the Greeks and Latins and the vulgar writers also said about composition, since it appears to me that what I have said is sufficient or at least gives light to what I have seemed to leave out) are these which, if sowed in the work with measure in time and place by the poet of Romances, will give life to the work, moving the emotions and putting actions and manners in the reader's view, just as if he should see them with his eyes. These make him see a wife's mourning her husband's departure or his death, as if one had seen the hand-to-hand combat and heard the outcry. These show a mother's joy in seeing her little son out of danger, as if one should see her heart laid bare. These make us hear the father's reproofs of his little son, as if we should have before our eyes the severity of that grave face full of tender indignation and have put into our ears those words full of loving threat. These make us see the leaders command, the people obey, the soldier go to war, the sages advise and foresee, the lover complain, entreat, and promise; the loved lady, coy, beautiful, wantonly gay, chary in glances, sparing in words, feigning to be distant and to be coy about showing herself, and ever to suspend the lover between hope and fear. These put tempests before our eyes, make us see the lightning, hear the thunder, fear the wrath of the stormy sea with those among the reefs and the billows. These make us see cities turn to rubble, put before our eyes the flames spreading through the temples, the towers, and private houses, make us hear the roofs falling in, the shrieks of the impoverished and unfortunate people, make us see mothers clasp their children to their bosoms with loving cries; the spoilers in contrast joyously loot the temples of the immortal gods and the homes of the citizens, and on every side the enchained prisoners run away. These make us see the snows fall white, the fields bloom, the grainfields wave, the rivers flow. These move and quieten our minds, arouse us to wrath and to feel pity; draw sighs from our breast, fill our eyes with tears; and make those who know how to use them become masters of our minds. Finally, these bring us living things, pulsing, breathing before our eyes. Although I have always known myself to be far from this excellence and perfection in composing, nevertheless I have always sought for such virtue in my writings, if not fully expressed, at least suggested so as to indicate that if I had not carried them out well, at least I had recognized them and intended to effect them with all study and diligence. I have always intended to do this, as have those to whom a similar intention is of no small importance in a matter of such great moment.

Now that we have not only put together but also enlivened this essay on the writer of Romances, we should perhaps be able, Messer Giovambattista, to arrive at our conclusion and to draw to an end what has been said. But since I am eager to give you more than you asked for, if not in quality, at least in quantity, I have not judged it extraneous to what has been written to add some other things. Though these matters are not on the subject of the structure and composition of a poem; nevertheless, in order to polish it and to know its defects (if any), these will be of no little aid to one who will not scorn to consider them and put them into practice.

Therefore, since nature did not make our minds less diverse than our faces and no one of us is apt in all things, the poet ought first to test himself to see to what his nature inclines and what is the strength of his genius, and whether his forces are sufficient for his shoulders to support so great a burden. Having known by experience that he is sufficient to the heavy weight, he should be able to undertake his poem. Certainly the composition of Romances is different from that of a sonnet or a madrigal or a canzone and is not for every man, as those who think that, by bedaubing papers with ink, they have completely achieved the excellence of poetry. Poor indeed are those papers and miserable those ink blots that are used by such crude hands with such defamation.

None can be equal to such a work, Messer Giovambattista, who is not of a most lively and versatile genius and, like a chameleon, capable of taking on all colors that surround him. Besides being disposed by nature, he does this by being well versed in the disciplines and languages and by devoting days and nights to the better poets, and by exercising himself variously before he undertakes a work of such importance that it may not merit in this language less than the heroic compositions in Greek and Latin. After the poet has done this and has discovered he is fit for such an undertaking, he will then set out to compose. Our imperfection is such that no one man, no matter how learned, practiced, ingenious, and judicious, can see all that belongs to perfection in composition. Our imperfection is attended by the feeling that naturally carries the author to his matter and also becomes greater, so that it often appears deceitful to his eyes and makes him little less than blind to it. It is of the greatest aid to the poet to submit what he has composed to another's judgment and, having laid aside his own convictions, to accept the criticism of learned men with respect not only to thoughts and feelings, which are wholly of invention, but also to all things we discussed above, which do not have to do with passions and feelings and so need only to be viewed as to what in them is displeasing in beauty. Furthermore these critics may see skillfully the obscure among the splendid parts, the dark among the light, and the flaws made by the poet among the perfect, who is overcome, as we said, by feelings and having entered into the poem in all its aspects, of

The Requisites of a Poet

which each so engages him that his judgment, necessarily scattered in many places, fails him.

It is true that great care ought to be taken not to show his writings to one who is hard of hearing or has bleared eyes or to one who has one thing in his heart, another in his mouth, and delights more in flattery than in the truth; but to one with ears, chaste, purged, and accustomed to smoothness and harmony of verse; who has sight sharper than a lynx, who has a mind and spirit so candid that he would hold in horror the committing of the great crime he would commit if he should speak less than the truth, as I know many do, those who often praise an author's works in his presence, then as soon as they have left him, laugh at them and scoff at him, reveling in their worst manner at having deceived him; thus deluded with the notion that he ought to be praised extravagantly, he exposes himself to being ridiculed by everyone.

A Poet Must Seek Criticism That happy spirit Ariosto, truly born to this kind of poetry,‡‡‡ was accustomed to seeking advice for his writings from men of letters, especially from those excellent in composition in this language and, following their judgment, often revised, omitted, added, modified. It was his custom first to see (before anything was said to him) if he could discover what those to whom he submitted his verses would find lacking in him. These men were accustomed therefore to point out exactly and indeed rigorously what seemed to them to need correction; then they left him to think about it. If he was satisfied as to what they would like him to do, he did not inquire further.§§§ If not, he would heed their opinion and if it pleased him, he accepted it; if not, he remained of his own opinion.

The poet should certainly not bind himself with others' judgment so as to be lost in it and only adhere to what anyone may judge of his works; but he should accept only that judgment which is inherently amicable, mature, and accompanied by doctrine and experience; he should not accept the judgment of those who have certain caprices by which they judge, as those made yellow-eyed by an excess of bile and thus know no other color than what they have in their eye. These reject everything that does not agree with their distorted judgment; thus anyone who believes them too much often spoils his artistry and chooses the imperfect instead of the excellent.

I have discovered it to be profitable for a work when the composer laid it aside for some time and turned to composing another work, then taking up the former work again, considered it diligently. His original fervor and love for it when it was born—almost as if it were a new child—having cooled off, the author sees it as if it were not his own, so that he finds in it much to correct which his original fervor had not permitted him to see. This he should do not just once, but many times; the oftener he will devote himself to it, the better his work will become.

Danger in Over-revision — Certainly he should avoid excessive use of the file, so that the good is lost along with the bad; as someone said, he ought to know when to lift his hand from the desk, because, as I have often said, excess is bad in any undertaking.

I have also found rewriting to be of the greatest use, since one pays more attention to what he writes than to what he reads, and the hand, the minister of the intellect, greatly aids the writer's genius. Many who have avoided this profitable labor have left imperfect writing that perhaps would have been perfected if they had not left it unrevised. In writing and rewriting much more remains with us than in reading, since the hand with the pen must form every letter and join together every word over some space of time, during which the intellect and the judgment can perform their function better than in reading; the eye runs over more often what the hand does. Rewriting is thus the reason why many things lacking are added and many excessive things are taken out.

The Poet Seeks Knowledge The composer is also aided by conversing with the practitioners of those arts he is to treat, as with the doctors, of the body's health and the structure of its members and their nature; with the learned men, of the affairs of state; with the astronomers; with the geographers, of the earth, of the sea, of the rivers, and of voyages; with the naturalists, of the beginnings of things and of their generation; with mariners, of the arts of navigation; with the captains, of war, of ordnance, and of feats of arms; with cavaliers, of steeds and jousts; with princes, of ruling peoples and cities; and (not to go into more detail) with all those whose arts he will need in writing. All that is in nature being a fit subject for the poet, and no less that which belongs to the liberal and mechanic arts, it would be too burdensome to learn all this before beginning to write. He will therefore need to consult those who have studied such things and have practiced them a great deal.¶¶¶

The poet will also be aided in doing what Leonardo da Vinci, that most excellent painter, was accustomed to do. Whenever he would paint some figure, he considered first its quality and its nature, i.e., whether it tended to be noble or plebeian, joyous or grave, troubled or gay, old or young, of irate or tranquil mind, good or evil; and then, knowing its being, he went where he knew persons of such quality congregated and observed diligently their faces, manners, clothes, and bodily movements. Having found that which seemed to him suitable to what he wished to create, he put it down with his stylus in the little book he always carried in his waistband. He did this repeatedly; then, when he had gathered as much as he judged was needful for the image he wished to paint, he set about shaping it and succeeded marvelously in doing so. Though he did this in all his works, he did it with all diligence in the table he painted in Milan in the convent of the preaching friars, in which is imaged our Redeemer with his disciples at their meal.

My father, Messer Christophoro, a most judicious and articulate man, used to tell me, when he frequently discussed composition with me, that Da Vinci, having finished the picture of Christ and eleven of the disciples, painted the body of Judas as far as the head, but went no further. The friars complained to the Duke, who was to pay Da Vinci a large price for the painting. The Duke, having heard the brothers' complaint, summoned Leonardo and asked him why he had delayed for so long the completion of the painting. Da Vinci replied that he wondered at his Excellency's complaining about it, because not a day passed that he did not spend two whole hours on it.

The Duke was satisfied with these words, but the friars continued to complain about Da Vinci's slowness. The Duke told them that he had talked with Da Vinci, who had told him that he spent two hours every day on the painting. The friars replied that only Judas's head remained

How Leonardo da Vinci Worked

to be done, that all the other images were completed; that considering the time he had spent in doing the other heads, if he worked two hours a day as he had told the Duke, the whole painting would be finished; but that for more than a year it had stood without a hand put on it.

The exasperated Duke then summoned Da Vinci and with troubled face said to him, "What is this these friars tell me? You tell me not a day passes that you do not put in two hours on the painting; they say to me that for more than a year you have not been in their convent." Da Vinci replied, "What do these friars know about painting? True, as they say, I have not gone there for a long time; but they do not speak the truth when they say I do not spend at least two hours every day on this picture." Said the Duke, "How can this be if you do not go there?" Then DaVinci, almost laughing, replied, "Your Excellency, I still have to do the head of Judas, the great traitor, as you know; he deserves to be depicted with as villainous a face as possible. Though I could have had many among those who accuse me remarkably like Judas; nevertheless, so as not to embarrass them by their likeness, every morning for more than a year, I have gone to the suburbs where live all the vile and ignoble persons, for the most part wicked and criminal, only to see if I should chance to behold a face fit to complete the portrait of that wicked man. I have not yet been able to find it, but as soon as it appears to me I shall finish what I have set out to do. Or if perchance I should not find it I could use as remarkably suitable that of this father prior who now so molests me." The Duke laughed at these last words of Da Vinci and was content with what he had said; having known with what judgment Da Vinci created his figures, he was not surprised that this painting became so excellent in the eyes of the world.

One day after this episode Da Vinci caught sight of a man who had a face to his liking; he quickly took his pencil, roughly sketched it, and with this and others that he had collected diligently for a year from various faces of vile and wicked people, he went to the friars and finished painting Judas, with such a face as appeared to have treachery engraved on its forehead. The poet ought to do likewise when he strives with the colors of writing to present the appearances, the customs, the conversations, the actions of diverse persons because he will not be able to draw thence the incredible except as the useful.

It will also be quite profitable to him to seek freely men's judgment, and he will achieve this if he will do with his writings as it is said Apelles did with his figures: He placed them without signature before the eyes of the world, so that, being more open to everyone's judgment, he would hear from many sources what everyone was saying about him; in this manner he learned about his faults and his virtues. *A Way to Get Objective Criticism*

It is no less useful to the poet sometimes to offer to others a number of stanzas that he may be pleased to clothe in others' garments and to expose them as ornate and pompous in another's attire. These verses being read under the name of such a one who is reputed to know how to do anything but stanzas, the author will not doubt that his name causes him to be judged with respect. And being hidden under the cloak of another's ignorance, he hears what he wishes about his writing; if his stanzas are praised, he laughs to himself at him who struts in another's clothes and swells with those compliments he knows are not really his. But indeed the author should not overdo this. Twenty-five or even fifty stanzas can be offered in order to hear freely how they appear to others, but to offer a hundred of them is indeed to pay too dearly, since to proceed so far demands much time and effort, and it sometimes happens that thoughts are repeated in them. Finding that he had lightly given them to such a one, he could say of him what Vergil said of his *Thyestes*, attributed to another: "It was (if you do not know) my goat, and Damon himself confessed to me it was but said he could not pay it back."[199] So he had to let him keep the verses. If indeed he is compelled to tell him, he will tell him much less happily than he had done before. This leaves in one's mind a great aversion, as anyone who has had the experience can testify.

These are the things, Messer Giovambattista, which I had in mind concerning the composition of Romances. I have written them down as well as my affairs, public and private, have allowed me. Such as they are, I offer them to you with my affection for you, which has always made me regard you not only as a dear pupil but also as a son. If I have come up to what you wished, I shall rejoice over my labors. If not, I shall be pleased to have made clear to you that, although the task you set for me was hard and laborious, nevertheless the good will I have for you enabled my shoulders to bear the heavy load, with the desire to treat the subject less than adequately in trying to please you rather than not to treat it at all and so deny you what you asked of me. May our Lord bless and prosper your studies, that you may be equal to the esteem in which men hold you; and I, seeing the fruit of my labors already abundant in you, can rejoice fully.

29 April 1549.

APPENDIX

* It should be noted, nevertheless, that Plato in the third of *Laws* believes that not only the laudable deeds of great men were sung but also their wicked deeds. . . . I believe it happens that the romancers at times detest . . . and shun them as vicious and unworthy of the noble mind of the cavalier.

† It is too indecent to propose another insipid, foul subject . . . or one impossible for imitation, not fit for art. This is an error, that does not deserve pardon, one that Aristotle called an error *per se*, i.e., one involving the substance of poetry. This kind of error is quite different from the error *per accidente*, which occurs in material not central to the poetry. If a poet should set out to describe a palace and err in some part of the architecture, his error would be excusable, since this is outside the realm of his art. Likewise, if the poet should describe the structure of a galley and err in its equipment and armament, his error would be pardonable. But an error involving the subject of which his poem is born is not excusable.

‡ . . . honored and worthy of eternal memory, since . . . life, before they were praised, as Petrach said very wisely: "La vita il fine, il di loda la sera"; nor was this said because he wished to consider human happiness or unhappiness, as did Solon, of whose thought Aristotle spoke in the first of *Ethics* in the tenth chapter; and Petrarch himself (setting aside for the moment what Ovid said about it in the third of the *Metamorphoses*) in the sonnet beginning: "Se col cieco desir, che il cor distrugge" [*Canzoniere*, No. 56]. But this should be understood with respect to praise or blame, which precede custom, as we shall speak of in its place. Speeches of praise . . . made after death or also praises given in history . . . or in a poem . . . of a person's actions . . . are without suspicion of adulation . . . that was said by the wiser that the adulator is worse than the enemy, and that adulation is a veil under which the sweetness of false praise . . . kill men who receive it for true praise. The panegyrics of Pliny and of Ausonius similarly were not without great blame. . . . The *Panegyrics* of Claudian were judged to be made in praise of men of these times, since these works were not heroic poems, i.e., woven with the thread that ought to order a regular poem worthy of the name heroic, but were rather . . . in the congregations of people (from whom they took the name) on

Giraldi's Notes

the days of solemn feasts. Praise also belongs to the epithalamia made for nuptials . . . of newlyweds to give good omens of children to be born and to show that they cannot be born to them unless the parents are worthy issue of their fathers in whose praise the epithalamium was composed . . . form of the heroic poems . . . nevertheless had learned from many authors who have set the standards for composing them artistically. But although not from the actions of a living man . . . nevertheless it is possible in the right time and place to praise in the poem a living gentleman or cavalier, as Vergil brought into the shield of Aeneas, described in the eighth of the *Aeneid*, the praise of Augustus and Agrippa.

§ These are not without grace and are very pleasing to the hearers when used in the proper place and time in our language; nevertheless they are far from a serious subject.

¶ Which is shown us by Bembo with rare examples of composition and observation of fitting language.

** If one who follows such a judicious philosopher can be said to err.

†† Each of these styles has its own fittingness and excellence in ornament.

‡‡ This furor is a kind of celestial inspiration that lights up the rational mind and fills it with a divine spirit. Ennius therefore said that poets are not sane, agreeing perhaps with Plato. . . . The mind is touched by a sane fury . . . and divinely inflamed. Not without reason did the great author [Ovid] say of it: "Est Deus in nobis agitante calescimus illo" [*Fasti*, 6.5].

But, granted that without this spirit infused in our mind good poetic writing could not be, its virtue is of little or no avail unless it is accompanied by intelligence. There is no reason for thinking that the immortal gods give us their gifts if we twiddle our thumbs; therefore Euripides said the gods aid those who act. Those who believe this spirit infused in us may make us write things about which we do not know are much deceived. There is need to study and compare well; *exercitatio*, aided by divine grace . . . and of study and of grace granted to him. Therefore the better judges . . . Horace showed this artfully . . .

§§ Not only Homer but Plato also, in the two first dialogues of *Laws*, wrote of wine and drunkenness. And on either subject he was so diffuse in showing the ancient uses of wine and drink that he used up, I ought not to say uselessly, a good part of each of his . . .

¶¶ Homer often presents the gods as if they were mortals and goddesses and queens as if they were common people.

*** As Eracliense, the father of Roman eloquence, wrote of Zeuxis, these were brought together by the admirable mastery of a learned hand into the harmonious unity of a beautiful body.

††† Servius's opinion about this ought to be included. He says Sandyx was an herb called Varana by the peasants—a glaring blunder in interpreting Vergil.

‡‡‡ And to have long memories of the great and excellent; as Vergil said, "Et meministis enim Divoe, et memorare potestis" [*Aeneid*, VII, 645].

For Pages 9 to 52

§§§ In his account of the destruction of Troy, Vergil also feigned Pyrrhus as killing Priam. In the lines, "Jacet ingens litore truncus, / avulsumque umeris caput, et sine nomine corpus" [*Aeneid*, II, 557-58], Vergil had in mind the death of Pompey. Moreover, Pyrrhus was too young to have done this deed. The story goes that Achilles, his father, clothed as a young girl, was given to Licomede, who thought he was a girl and put him with her daughter Deidamia. Achilles deceived Deidamia, and when Ulysses discovered him and took him to Troy, Deidamia was left pregnant with Pyrrhus, who was born while Achilles was at the siege of Troy.

¶¶¶ At the same time the poet makes many other things stand out, such as tempests, battles, batterings-down, sieges, feats of arms, legations, parleys, contentions, descriptions of countries, of temples, of official positions, and of persons. The poet should put in these and similar things so skillfully that they are integrated with the primary action and depend on it, in that these happen either before or after or at the same time as the primary action. For achieving this the poet received the greatest praise, since this function to please reader or hearer very much relieves the satiety which a long continued narration of the main action could create, if unbroken by any delightful interpolations.

* The subject of the work was called the fable because the poet does not deal in things as they are but as they ought to be and so changes history and makes it become a fabulous creation, of greater worth indeed than if he had treated the subject factually. Feigning or fabling is necessary to convey an idea either of a perfect man or of a perfect action since the frailty of human nature obstructs human perfection; nor are our actions on the whole perfect. Therefore feigning this or that detail is necessary to put before another's eyes either a perfect man or a perfect action. Though this perfection cannot be found in the factual, it can be feigned and presented to the view, not by speaking falsities but by elevating men to a better state in which they can be challenged to distinguish action, so that they may approach as nearly as possible to the perfection the writer envisages. This kind of subject enables writers to achieve immortality in their poems.

† Vergil showed this well in the death of Turnus, who had broken the covenants arrived at by the authority of the immortal gods and killed many Trojans in his atrocities, since the poet reserved punishment for Turnus in the duel with Aeneas. In this

Giraldi's Notes

duel it was of no avail for him to yield to Aeneas to save his life, since it seemed contrary to justice for Aeneas to let a wicked man live. So justice prevailed over clemency. Even though Turnus prayed for mercy, Aeneas noted he was wearing the sword-belt of Pallas, whom Turnus had killed. The death of his dear friend and of the other Trojans contrary to the pledged word and the covenants ordained by the intervening of the immortal gods returned to Aeneas' memory; therefore [he judged] that as punishment Turnus deserved death. "Immolat et poenam scelerato ex sanguine sumit" [*Aeneid*, XII, 949]. Aeneas could not pardon Turnus for having killed Pallas in battle contrary to the covenants; and though his enemy had yielded to him, Turnus had broken faith with him and the gods themselves; therefore Aeneas was less piteous than just.

‡ Vice alone is enough to make man unhappy; thus the divine Plato said in the *Alcibiades* that only the wise (since no wise man is vicious) are happy, all ignorant rascals unhappy, since vice comes out of ignorance; so all the ignorant are evil. Even though in common thought those are unhappy to whom things happen against their desires, these, if virtuous, ought not to be called unhappy but unfortunate.

§ He ought to do this in such a way that it has the spice of pleasure; if he always concentrates on the serious, the pitiable, the terrible, his composition will be unpleasing and a departure from the first principle that it should delight. Therefore he makes it his business to choose the middle way, so that by uniting the useful and virtuous with the delightful he will reach the goal which Horace said he achieves who mingles the useful with the sweet. This joining the pleasant with the useful has been of such importance to those who have known the best of human affairs and have said that the more the poet pleases the less he is a philosopher. The philosopher treats serious and excellent matter with gravity, but the poet by his art treats the same things with pleasure.

¶ These were composed at the time the Pope had his seat in Avignon; he intended to show that whereas Rome used to be entirely in religion and holiness while in her was seated the Christian catholic church, so after it was transferred to another place, Rome had become a harborage for all the vices.

** In this respect Trissino in his *Italia* was shown to be less the poet in what was fitting.

†† In this respect Vergil was marvelous for the description of the temple of Apollo in the sixth book and for that of the Latins in the seventh. Ovid amplified this in the house of the sun [*Metamorphoses*, II, 1-30], and although he shows in this the liveliness of his genius, nevertheless he is less grand. Claudian describes the house of Venus artistically in the epithalamium of Honorius

and Maria. The poets of the Romances have followed these last two. But Petrarch [in *The Triumph of Love*] preferred to follow Vergil rather than Ovid and Claudian in describing the place where Venus had her dwelling. Though he did not devote many verses to the dwelling, nevertheless by ornamental images and by grandeur and by attention to the pantings that are experienced in loving, he employed opposites with effective art, just as Vergil, to show the antiquity and the illustrious works of Latin kings, conveyed in a most serious manner the names and likenesses of kings and the trophies associated with their victories [*Aeneid*, VII, 170-91].

‡‡ To give a general rule about what pertains to gravity, as regards the subject, there are the introductions of the gods, the descriptions of celestial places, things relating to the great captains, how they make war, their strategy and councils, their deliberations and other such things . . . the descriptions, especially of storms, of deeds of arms, of sieges and similar things make the heroic poem serious . . . in these things, however the judicious writer ought to avoid . . . I do not say this because they do not sometimes occur in heroic poetry so that they do not reach that grandeur of style belonging to the most serious stories; but the . . . poet should pay attention to the subject and treat it so that it is not unseemly. . . . Vergil described Venus as wearing a huntress's habit and fitted the words to the subject. This description was in more humble mode than that of Camilla, who had on a warrior's habit and was a captainess of war; both of them were fittingly described. . . .

§§ In introducing his persons, the poet ought to consider carefully what they are prone to do and to suffer. In doing so, he will find useful a knowledge of the differences in nations and in natures, the manners of life, usages, and customs; and the management of affairs and the power of those whom he will bring in . . . Aristotle discussed these things copiously in his *Rhetoric* and Horace compressed them briefly in his *Satires* when he discussed poetry.

¶¶ I know some wretched wits whose ears are not tuned to smoothness and elegance have held that breaking the smoothness and putting the pause in the line out of the order we have mentioned is a more graceful manner of composing. But since mature judgments and the better compositions show how wrong this seems, I leave them in the opinion in which they persevere rather than contradict them . . . I shall not say superfluous but vain efforts, since ancient and modern writers who have made their names immortal answer them in my stead, and the writings of those who have Midas's ears give ample testimony of their wrong opinion.

*** He ought to be wary nevertheless . . . goddess is called . . . mortal lady . . . therefore Petrarch said in the first capitolo of *The Triumph of Death*, "Vattene in pace o vera mortal dea." . . . But

For Pages 52 to 105

Giraldi's Notes

despite all this Petrarch did not give the name goddess to his lady until after her death, as reads the sonnet, "Quel che di odore, e di color vincea" [*Canzoniere*, No. 337], "Il mio signor sedersi, e la mia dea." In saying this of the death of his lady, he intended to say that his lady was already deified, that she had already passed to another life. One must consider that this religious and truly Christian author, in speaking of the Virgin Mother, gave her the name of goddess . . . it seemed to him that this name of god belonged solely to the majesty of the Highest. . . .

††† We spoke earlier of the word *diva* and showed it was never employed of a living woman by a recognized writer either ancient or modern and that there are those who would favor this bad usage, and stated that it is commonly so used by lovers and noted that the word is not badly used by Ariosto. I say further that whoever examines the origin of this word, i.e., from the Latin *divus (diva)*, will see that the regular writers of the Latin language who wrote before the language had fallen from its majesty, as it began to fall after the emperor Octavian, never used *divus* or *diva* of a living person. Cicero so named Julius Caesar in his second Philippic after Caesar's death; Vergil, speaking of Camilla who was living, would not call her *diva* since he ought not to use the word of a living woman, but called her Dia Camilla. If one should quote what Vergil said of Octavian in the line, "Nec tam presentes alibi cognoscere Dives" [*Eclogue* I, 41], and say that indeed Octavian was then living, I would answer that the emperors of the time were held as sainted and divine and, indeed, Octavian was the first to be called σεβαστὸς [*sebastos*], which signifies as worthy of being worshiped. So it happened that Tityrus said that Octavian would always be god to him and that he would often sacrifice lambs on his altars [*Eclogue* I, 6-8]. Thus we see that Vergil said this of one deified in life, not of a simple mortal. But leaving to their own opinion these stubborn people who would have vulgar usage prevail over the authority of the excellent writers, I believe nevertheless that the better judges prefer the authority of those who know and not the bad usage of the vulgar, from which come all imperfections. As for this the authority of Ariosto can be appealed to, his work in this respect, as in others, being full of various lights of genius and of doctrine, so it will not be allowed to another who seeks to acquire reputation by his compositions. If perhaps he should not undertake a long work or be completely censurable by showing himself (as Horace says) somewhat dull, it should not be permitted either in a sonnet or in a canzone if one would not like to be compared to Panfilisassi or Serafione or Sassiferrati or others loathsome even in name. Although I have noted this word *diva*, and other things, in Ariosto, I should not be eager to change anything in his work, for I see too many

who have undertaken the task to vary many things in the last edition of his *Furioso*, claiming authority and authenticity for their caprices from M. Galasso, the author's brother, saying they had from him a book of proofs in which were corrections not only of the spelling but of many other things. This is simply not true. In addition to the testimony I could offer as one who was very close to this noble author, the very diligence he showed over the last edition before he published it testifies that when the work was issued, he had made absolutely all the corrections he intended.

For Pages 105 to 108

I say this because I know (Ariosto having talked with me many times about it) that he reserved the five cantos he had in hand to add to his work in case he should have it reprinted, not to prolong the work but to make a new poem and to interpose them in the work (if death had not cut him off) where it would have seemed best to him, as we see he interposed many details, even whole cantos, in the second edition, but not in the first. He intended to do this so that another new edition would bear not only a new imprint but also some new material that would make the work more pleasing for the originality inherent in it. If a commentator had seen the others before he had given them the final touches, he would have discovered many details to be criticized which were corrected by his fine taste. Ariosto would have been as equally diligent with the five cantos as he was with the first edition of the whole work. Such was his way of working. First he pondered and repondered his poem for sixteen years after the first edition; never a day passed in this whole time that he was not about this, both with pen and with reflection. When he had revised to the point that seemed fitting to him, in both the additions and the corrections, he took it to many fine, talented Italians to get their judgment—men like Bembo, Molza, Navagero, and others whom he mentioned in the last canto—and having had their opinions, he went back home. As Apelles was accustomed to do about his painting, so Ariosto did about his work; indeed, two years before he let it go to the printer, he placed it in the hall of his house and let it be judged by anyone who read it. Finally, having had so much criticism both within the city and without, he took it into account as seemed best to him.

In this time arose Tolomei's and some others' superstition of omitting the aspirate H from the words of our language which from ancient usage were accustomed to have it and had carried it with them both from the Greek and the Latin. Ariosto seems clearly to laugh at this, saying that such people had learned their manner of writing from cobblers, smiths, barbers, and other such low people; not knowing the law of writing, they write as if ignorance were guiding them and so leave off the H where it rightfully should be. And he used to say that those who leave the H off *huomo* are not

Giraldi's Notes

recognizable as *uomo*; those who leave if off *honore* are not worthy of *onore*. And if Hercules should see them leaving it off his name, he would attack the culprits and strike them over the head with a mazzard. With such jokes he mocked the inventors of this superstition, especially seeing that they leave it in other words as proper and not foreign to the Tuscan dialect. He would never accede to this superstitious diligence, since it seemed to him (as it ever has to me, and still appears, and will appear, and so I have completely freed myself of it) that Bembo, Molza, Navagero, Sannazaro, and other excellent writers of his time judged much better; these have left it off, not through negligence but through judgment, from the words borrowed from Greek and Latin which had been adopted in the Tuscan language. On the other hand he would never leave it off words that by their nature ought to have it, as *huomo, honore, humile, honesto, hoggi, hora,* and others like them. Nor would he ever write *Febo, Filosofo,* and other such words derived from Latin and Greek, but always *Phebo, Philosopho,* as can be seen in the book he himself had printed at Ferrara by Francesco Ferrarese da Valenza; to its correction he attended faithfully while it was being printed. This printing was begun in 1532 in the month of May and was finished in the month of September of the same year. During this correction of the printing he contracted the illness that led to his death, to the common sorrow of all men and all noble spirits, in the year 1534 on the sixth of July.

Now I leave this for the thought of judicious men, not to mention the true testimony that Ercole Bentivoglio can offer, who was with Ariosto constantly, and much loved and honored by him for his strength of character; and that I can also offer, as if of his household and as one who was always present with him in his infirmity. After Lodovico Bonacciuolo, doctor of great reputation and learning, he was under the excellent Giovanni Manardi and the learned Antonio Maria Canani. I already had my doctor's degree and conferred with them. From the beginning they diagnosed as incurable the sickness that tormented him for over a year. So I leave to good judgment how far from the truth is the notion that he undertook to revise the printed work on which he had labored so hard for sixteen years, as we said above, in view of the fact it had just been printed and he was so ill and passed on to a better life. How presumptuous he can be said to be who was avid to change the work of so distinguished an author, so carefully composed and printed, as to put in it his own capricious forms far from the author's mature judgment.

I could here note much as badly changed, but since this will require another time and another composition I shall confine myself to speaking of Ariosto himself. But I shall note two among the many to show what the others are like. One that this undergraduate commentator regarded as a puerile grammatical error in Ariosto is *al specchio*. I need not write that he says that *il* is never found when the following word begins with *s* followed by another consonant; then *lo* always occurs, never *il*. I do not know how this ingenuous annotator came to let such a statement fall from his pen. The usage occurs in Petrarch, a most careful writer, as all the old manuscript texts and the printed ones based on them testify. An example: "Io nol diro, perche poter no'l spero"; and another: "Essendo il spirto gia da lei diviso." All the good texts, both manuscript and printed, not corrupted by anyone else's superstition show this usage.

For Page 108

In these places we see that although generally he observed the adopted rule about *il*, he did not avoid in the two verses cited putting the article *il* with the words *spero* and *spirto*, to show that this was contrary to the ancient usage of the language. So we see it is contrary to the author's intention to change *al specchio* to *a specchio*; the latter is never used by writers of reputation.

This commentator quotes another line, "Mirabil voci e solazzevol balli," and says the usage is contrary to that of the good writers of the language, since the *i* was omitted from words plural in number as always required and that in this Ariosto violated the common usage of the language. To this objection one can reply that he wrote so with the authority of the most careful writer of the Tuscan language, namely, Petrarch, from whom the rules and usages of this most beautiful language are drawn. One reads in this purest and chastest of writers in the canzone, "Una donna piu bella assai che'l sole" [*Canzoniere*, No. 119], "Con voce allor di si mirabil tempre"; and in the sonnet that begins, "Chi vuol veder quantumque può natura" [No. 248], "Giunti in un corpo con mirabil tempre." And in the first capitolo of *The Triumph of Love* he wrote: "E di lacciuoli innumerabil carco, / Vien catenato Giove innanzi al carro." In these citations one can see that Petrarch abbreviated such words by leaving off the *i*. Ariosto wrote so, not through ignorance nor through following the vulgar linguistic usage, but with such authority that it would be better to err with him than to follow these superstitious people who assume so much it would seem one ought to take for oracles what falls from their pens or mouths.

To conclude this matter: It should be more than clear to any judicious reader that Ariosto should be left within the bounds of that which he had published with so much labor, especially since he himself was the corrector of the printing; and that it is a myth trumped up by a commentator that just after his work had been lifted from the presses, he went about new corrections. This fellow invented the tale to give authority to his fantastic notions. The alleged tale, that as soon as the book was printed he put himself to revising it, is obviously far from the truth; immediately after the

Giraldi's Notes

edition he went into a long and serious illness, as we said. Of this we have said enough: It is time we return to the observations on words.

‡‡‡ At this point I do not think I am digressing in calling the writer's attention to the apostrophe as a device contributing to smooth sound. It is to be used with great care, not, as I see it, used every day by many. Every time a word ends in a vowel and the following begins with a vowel, they omit the vowel from the first and put the apostrophe in its place. In our language this often distorts the thought. As this occurs when the vowels are omitted from various words, it also often occurs with respect to the articles. Indeed I think that sometimes the clash of the vowels makes a harsh sound and (as the Latins say) gives birth to a hiatus if the vowel ending the word is left off. But when this does not occur, the ear is not offended if the whole word is left. It would be bad in every way not to leave off the vowel after the article in this verse: "Lo alto Signor, dinanzi a cui non vale," since pronouncing *lo alto* impedes the smoothness of the verse and slows up the felicitous flow it has if so offered: "L'alto Signor, dinanzi a cui non vale." But it would not be so bad to omit the vowels occurring in this verse: "Le stelle, il cielo e gli elementi a prova." This verse is to be preferred in this way: "Le stell', il ciel e gl'elementi a prova." One can see therefore that the apostrophe is not to be used if it impedes the smoothness of the utterance. I leave this to the writer's judgment and shall say that the apostrophe should be used as sparingly in prose as in verse.... To turn now to discuss the choice of words, let me say that, assuming that one needs to study the principles of the use of words for elegant and dignified verse and that the choice of them is always to be commended and that much ought to be pointed out about the subject, nevertheless the laws of this sort of poetry are not so strict that words cannot be chosen which are not in the books of the great ancient writers; in fact, words in everyday use and selected from the better form of speaking can be used judiciously in compositions.

§§§ It happened therefore that Ariosto in his *Furioso* went beyond the laws pertaining to sonnets and canzoni, and indeed the commentator ought to be content with what he did with wise judgment ... and indeed he intended to devote some judgment to the position of this ... viewed and reviewed, and placed before the judgment of so many able men, [the commentator] ought not to change or twist what the author wished to leave as it was.

¶¶¶ Ariosto followed so closely in his footsteps that he seems not to move a step out of his tracks (I refer to the subject-matter) of that fine genius who, in those times before the resources of our beautiful language were known, was an admirable inventor of poetic fictions suitable to Romances. I should like to believe that if he had been living at the time Ariosto composed the *Furioso*, when the power of our language had been revealed, he would not have turned out to be less happy in metrical rhythm and quality of verse in his fabulous inventions of knights errant.

* Among these arise, nevertheless, some of enormous genius who choose to write . . . by rule and on this basis to compose well; as this comes out of little judgment, so it ought to be studiously avoided by judicious writers as erroneous and servile, since their rhymes are harsh to the reader because of the bad position of the words. . . .

† Nor can this consequence of imitation be called envy, since even if it is (as Aristotle says in the second of the *Rhetoric*) . . . displeasing to one mind not to have what another has, it does not cause pain to the one removed from the good of another . . . from this effect is born in a man the desire to make himself equal and to advance the one whom he sees to be greater than he in one way or another. As envy (which is a dislike of the good another deserves to have . . . so it is dislike of the felicity of those that unworthily have it) is worst of the vices, so emulation is a praiseworthy and virtuous desire to become like the one he set out to equal and to have for his own virtue, not out of malignity or by the wrong ways, the excellence he sees in another, without harm to him whom he seeks to equal or to surpass. . . .

‡ And indeed, in addition, not . . . any of the words that . . . and embellish the discourse, and the metaphor, either in verse or prose . . .

§ And if they are fit for the orator, they fit well in heroic and tragic compositions.

¶ And what Petrarch wrote: "April of the age" and "hair of the temples blooming before their time" and "golden hair silvered o'er" . . . with use of two metals in a metaphorical sense . . . .

** Here it is to be noted that these ought to be used in such a pleasing manner that the poet may not use them out of time or too frequently in his poem, so that if perchance he should be guilty of one of these two faults, where he sought to bring light into his composition, he would really achieve obscurity. I do not think I am off the subject to cite at this point the sources whence Aristotle would have metaphors derived. Metaphors, he says, come from four sources . . . they are drawn from the genus . . . as would be if . . . ugliness of anger . . . better dignifies the burning of anger, by metaphor of the burning of fire . . . to the quality of anger . . . intense cold . . . giving to cold the heat of fire . . . . The second is from the species to the genus . . . the third kind is from species to species, as it would be to say, he truncated the head with a sword,

For Pages 108 to 139

Giraldi's Notes

cutting through the sinews and the bones, since *truncate (troncare)* appears instead of *cut through (tagliare)* and vice versa, these genera are not true species; but they are so called according as they mean more or less, almost as in place of the genus and of the species. The last kind is by proportion, as if we should say, old age is the setting sun of life and the setting of the sun is the old age of the dawn; and as if one should say, genius blooms in youth and maturity bears fruit. Petrarch used this kind artfully when he said: "Ove nacque colei ch'avendo in mano / Mio cor in su il florir e in su il far frutto."

This metaphor of proportion is very useful to compositions and contributes directly to pleasure . . . the beauties of their ladies, naming the golden hair, ebony brows, starry eyes, pearly teeth, ruby lips, white and red cheeks like lilacs and roses, or roses white and crimson, as Petrarch said for a similitude:

> Se mai candide rose, con vermiglie
> In vasel d'oro vider gli occhi miei,
> Allor allor da vergine man colte;
> Veder pensaro il viso di colei,
> Ch'avanza tutte l'altre maraviglie
>
> [*Canzoniere*, No. 127, 6th stanza, lines 1-5]

Egidio arises in the stanzas . . . of his chases . . . metaphor intended to describe the whiteness and the . . . of cheeks. Nor was this without grace when he said . . . in which voyage . . . a compact between January and May . . . to infer that would fall . . . and the snow . . . in the praises, but in the censure often applying to the metaphor . . . precious, by which . . . is praised in what is desired, as one who said . . . the teeth of . . .

†† . . . on the person of a single hero . . . so to serve the custom, as have already said . . . the action of that he had set out to imitate, for example, the idea of a perfect. . . . This was not necessary for Homer in the *Odyssey*, since he did not make Ulysses act like the warriors in the *Iliad* . . . and although he made the games . . . death of Patroclus . . . it did not seem fitting to Vergil for the majesty of poetry . . . in the death of father Anchises in the last six . . . although he put in the death of Pallas in the last six and a most untimely [death] . . . nevertheless he was only . . . to what was fitting in that time.

‡‡ If they are used fittingly; and they are called adjuncts because they always join some property to the words that they accompany or some greater efficacy; as if we should say courageous knight, we declare the characteristic of the knight, which is his heart and daring, and besides we should say much more than if we simply said knight. We may lessen also at times, yet unskillfully, as if we should say coy *(acerbetta)* nymph and very bad *(schifosetta)* girl. Of these

adjuncts those have wonderful pleasantness in which the property of the thing they are joined to inheres, as black and humid night, calm day, tumultuous or tranquil sea; and those also which are of the nature of metaphor, as swift thought, burning desire; and besides those simple ones, compound ones are sometimes used, as delirious (*forsennato*), surpassed (*sormontato*), surprised (*sorpreso*); and many contrary to things they are joined to, giving marvelous grace in our language . . . .

For Pages 139 to 158

§§ Since this excessiveness . . . either vicious or unregulated; therefore it was not without reason that Plautus said, "Nimia omnia nimium exhibent negotium."

¶¶ Bitter sweet, benign evil, sorrowful play, pleasing pain, perfidious loyalty, faithful deception, proud humility, humble exaltation.

*** These two hyperboles used by Petrarch and by Strozza are usually called simple. Of these modes of excessive speech Aristotle puts as the first that which is . . . like this Petrarch used in showing swiftness of his thought: "Volo con l'ali del pensiero al cielo" [*Canzoniere*, No. 362, "I fly to the heavens on the wings of thought"], and similarly if one wished to . . . a youth's lack of prudence who had given to . . . two greedy harlots, saying to him: "Ben il ha condutto il tuo folle desire/Nel mar d'amor in tra Cariddi e Scilla" ["Thy foolish desire has indeed led thee in the sea of love between Charybdis and Scylla"]; Horace likewise said artfully in *Odes* 1.27: "Ah miser! / Quanta laborabas charybdi, / Digne puer meliore flamma!" ["Ah! Wretched one! In what a Charybdis art thou struggling, boy worthy of a better flame!"]. This kind of hyperbole is the more artistic as it has in it . . . and has inherent in it a diminution of the thing we are talking about . . .

††† This also occurs in the commentaries . . . of poets or of philosophers or of orators or of historians who always adduce them in the Greek language . . . we see that where Cicero needed to bring them in . . . always introduced them with Latin words. The commentators of reputation, such as Donatus, Servius, Asconius, Claudianus . . . Servius makes composition of the Greek poets . . . Vergil; but let us leave . . . and I shall turn to . . .

‡‡‡ Here in the last part of this discourse, I shall not be ashamed to repeat such a profitable recollection.

§§§ So it can be said that his poem includes the criticism of all the excellent writers at the time he published the second edition, with the seal of his own hand, as we said above, since the new corrections were written in his own hand otherwise than in the aforesaid edition . . . not . . . that this is a . . . done by whoever has . . . with feigned authority . . . to make in Ariosto what he never intended to admit into his poem. . . .

¶¶¶ Indeed I do not say this so that I may . . . treat the things . . . which occur in the handling of the action, speaking of the aforesaid things . . . therefore better able to set forth what he proposed to narrate part by part—all of which pertains to becoming a judicious poet.

NOTES

¹ Pietro Bembo (1470-1547), poet, prose writer, critic. Giraldi refers here particularly to Bembo's *Prose della volgar lingua*, the first book of which argues that Italian is to be preferred to Latin for literary use and that the language of Florence as used by Petrarch and Boccaccio is best for a literary medium.

² Giraldi refers to Allessandro Citolini's *Lettere in difesa della lingua volgare* (Venice, 1540), in which Citolini concurs with Bembo.

³ Vincenzo Maggi, scholar and critic, whose chief work, written with Bartolomeo Lombardi, published at Venice in 1550, was *In Aristotelis Librum De Poetica Communes Explanationes.*

⁴ Giraldi's earlier *Discorso intorno al comporre delle comedie et delle tragedie*, dated 25 April 1543.

⁵ *The Gallic War*, Bk. VI, sec. 14.

⁶ *Brutus*, xviii, 71.

⁷ Bk. IV, chap. ii, sec. 3 (Loeb ed., p. 330).

⁸ *Factorum et Dictorum Memorabilium Libri Septem* ("Seven Books of Memorable Deeds and Sayings").

⁹ *Poetics*, 1450a, 37-38.

¹⁰ *Poetics*, 1451b, 19-26.

¹¹ *Georgics*, III, 4-5. The text Giraldi followed varied from a modern text like the Loeb; e.g., where Giraldi reads *notus*, Loeb reads *dictus*. "Who knows not pitiless Eurystheus, or the altars of detested Busiris? Who has not told of the boy Hylas?"

¹² *Poetics*, 1451a, 15-36.

¹³ Plutarch, *Moralia*, "How the Young Man Should Study Poetry," 16 (Loeb ed., I, 82-83).

¹⁴ Greek rhetorician and philosopher who flourished in the 2d century A.D. He is sometimes confused with the historian Maximus, the teacher of Marcus Aurelius. The former was the author of 41 διαλέξεις.

¹⁵ Canani or Canano (1515-1579), anatomist of Ferrara who taught in the university there; his book *Muscalorum humani corporis picturata dissectio* (1541) is important in the history of anatomy.

¹⁶ *Poetics*, 1450a, 37-38.

¹⁷ *Ars Poetica*, 147-152.

¹⁸ *Ars Poetica*, 147.

Editorial Notes

[19] *Poetics*, 1451a, 15-36.
[20] The first part of Pausanias's *Description of Greece*.
[21] Latin poet whose epic *Punica* in seventeen books is on the second Punic war.
[22] *The Eleventh or Trojan Discourse*, 24-25 (Loeb ed. of *Discourses*, I, 464 ff.).
[23] To whom Giraldi dedicated and addressed his *Discorso . . . delle comedie et delle tragedie*.
[24] *Italia Liberata*, Bk. 24: ". . . e l'Ariosto/Col Furioso suo, che piace al vulgo." (*Tutte le Opere*, Verona, 1729, I, 262.)
[25] *Poetics*, 1460a, 11-26.
[26] The painting referred to is probably Raphael's *Parnassus*, in which, as Vasari says, "Homer . . . blind, his head lifted, pours forth his verses while a youth [one of the poets] at his feet writes them down as he sings" (*Vasari's Lives of the Artists*, ed. B. Burroughs, [New York, 1946], 224). A study of a reproduction of the *Parnassus* will show that, although Giraldi's interpretation of the painting may be a little strained, it is quite possible to read into it the meaning he states.
[27] Plotius Tucca and Varius Rufus, poets and friends of Vergil and Horace (cf. Horace's *Satire* I.5.40). They were Vergil's literary executors who ignored Vergil's instructions to burn the *Aeneid*.
[28] *Aeneid*, II, 567-88. In *Quaestio Virgiliana*, Franciscus Campanus examines these twenty-two lines in detail in his defense of Vergil's poem; see p. 58 below.
[29] Presumably Giraldi refers to Garci Rodriguez de Montalvo, *Los quatro libros del Virtuoso cavallero Amadis de Gaula*, first published in 1508. Bernardo Tasso's *Amadigi* did not appear until 1560, six years after the date of Giraldi's *Discorso*.
[30] *Poetics*, 1460b, 23-37—1461a, 1-9.
[31] Giraldi refers to Bk. V of the *Saturnalia* of Macrobius, which consists of a detailed comparison of the *Aeneid* with the Homeric poems, with extensive parallel passages, showing how closely the *Aeneid* is indebted to the *Iliad* and the *Odyssey*. The specific statement Giraldi had in mind is apparently: "In quibus Vergilius Homerici carminis majestatem non aequet" [Vergil does not equal the majesty of the Homeric poem]; cf. *Macrobii Ambrosii Aurelii Theodosii . . . In Somnium Scipionis*, Lib. II. *Saturnaliarum*, Lib. VII., Venetiis, MDLXX, p. 417.
[32] The Homeric poems are cited often, in comparison with the *Aeneid* in Servius' commentary (*Servii Grammatici qui feruntur in Vergilii Carmina Commentarii*).
[33] *Institutio Oratoria*, X, 85-87.
[34] *Natural History*, II, iv, 12, v.
[35] *Ibid.*, XXXV, vi, 23, xl (Loeb ed., IX, 290).

³⁶ *Ecloga* IV, 45. "Of its own will shall scarlet [*sandyx*] clothe the grazing lambs."
³⁷ *Aeneid*, II, 199-249.
³⁸ An account of the destruction of Laocoon's sons by serpents is in Quintus Smyraneus (Quintus of Smyrna or of Calabria), *The Fall of Troy*, XII, 444-97 (Loeb ed. by A. S. Way, 519-20). This is parallel to and, it seems, based on the *Aeneid*; modern scholars agree with Giraldi that Quintus "imitated" Vergil here.
³⁹ *Aeneid*, V, 362-484.
⁴⁰ *Aeneid*, IX, 168-449.
⁴¹ *Aeneid*, IX, 672-755.
⁴² *Aeneid*, I, 184-93.
⁴³ Herodotus, II, 32 (Loeb ed., I, 313).
⁴⁴ *Aeneid*, III, 692-715.
⁴⁵ *Metamorphoses*, Bk. XV.
⁴⁶ Poem No. LXIV.
⁴⁷ Coluthus or Colluthus, Greek epic poet of Lycopolis in the Egyptian *Thebaid*; flourished *ca.* A.D. 500; author of one extant poem, *The Rape of Helen*.
⁴⁸ There are several allusions to the marriage of Peleus and Thetis in Hesiod's works, e.g., in *The Epic Cycle*, "The Cypria," 5. Giraldi's statement that Catullus "translated" from Hesiod is exaggerated.
⁴⁹ *Metamorphoses*, IX, 306-23.
⁵⁰ *Metamorphoses*, III, 407-510.
⁵¹ *Metamorphoses*, I, 452 ff.
⁵² *The Deipnosophists*, VII, 281b-c.
⁵³ *Italia Liberata dai Gotti*, Bk. Four.
⁵⁴ *Poetics*, 1451b, 33-39.
⁵⁵ Mainly in parts of Cantos VI, VII, VIII, and X of *Orlando Furioso*.
⁵⁶ *Poetics*, 1460a, 11-36.
⁵⁷ Giraldi seems to have in mind particularly Giovanni Pontano's Latin eclogue *Lepidina*.
⁵⁸ Ll. 151-52.
⁵⁹ This statement is representative of the Renaissance interpretation of Aristotle.
⁶⁰ For Diodorus' statement about the superiority of history over poetry, see *The Library of History*, I, xxxii, 1-3 (Loeb ed., I, 8-11).
⁶¹ *Poetics*, 1451, 1-11.
⁶² This interpretation of Aristotelian catharsis occurs frequently among Renaissance critics.
⁶³ *Canzoniere*, No. 128.
⁶⁴ *Canzoniere*, Nos. 136, 137, 138.
⁶⁵ *The Triumph of Fame* is one that has a digression.

Editorial Notes

⁶⁶ *Stanze per la Giostra*, Bk. One.

⁶⁷ Giraldi refers to Egidio da Viterbo (*ca*. 1465-1532). Egidio's poem *La Caccia d'Amore* is cited specifically.

⁶⁸ The reference seems to be to Girolamo Benivieni's *Amore* (1500), an allegorical poem in imitation of Lorenzo de' Medici's *Selva d'Amore*.

⁶⁹ For discussion of the concept of *enargeia* in Renaissance criticism, see Baxter Hathaway, *The Age of Criticism: The Late Renaissance in Italy* (Ithaca: Cornell, 1962), *passim*; and A. H. Gilbert, *Literary Criticism: Plato to Dryden* (Cincinnati: American Book Co., 1940), 165, 453, 677.

⁷⁰ In *La Poetica*, VI Divisione, Trissino defines "enargia" as "un ponere la cosa quasi avanti gli occhi" (*Tutte le Opere* [Verona, 1729], II, 115). In the succeeding pages Trissino's copious detailing of what ought to be the substance of a poem leads one to the conclusion, as apparently it did Giraldi, that by *enargia* Trissino meant very minute detail.

⁷¹ Cf. *Ars Poetica*, 119-27.

⁷² *Poetics*, 1454a, 29-31.

⁷³ *Quaestio Virgiliana*. Campanus stated that his purpose was to absolve the great poet of the alleged negligence which Tucca, Varius, and others had accused him of. On pp. 238-45 of *Iani Parrhasii Liber de rebus per epistolam quaesitis . . . adjuncta est Francisci Campani Quaestio Virgiliana* (1567), the twenty-two lines of the episode of Aeneas' wrath against Helen (*Aeneid*, II, 567-88) are quoted and discussed.

⁷⁴ *Nicomachean Ethics*, III, vi, 10.

⁷⁵ Error for Melanippe.

⁷⁶ *The Deipnosophists*, XIV, 627a-c.

⁷⁷ Giraldi refers to Marco Girolamo Vida's *Christiad* (1535), VI, 884 ff. Vida was born at Cremona on the river Po. In this passage from the *Christiad*, God the Father prophesies that all the cities will resound with Christ's praises, particularly in Italy. One of the regions specified is where the Po, king of rivers, rushes on, threatening the walls of Cremona. There, after fifteen centuries, a poet will arise to sing Christ's glory. Giraldi errs slightly in writing that the Christ in Vida's poem prophesies this; actually the Father speaks these lines. But the point Giraldi makes is the impiety of Vida's putting in his poem a divine foretelling of Vida himself as the poet who will write of Christ.

⁷⁸ Giraldi apparently refers to Bartolomeo Ricci's *De Imitatione Libri Tres* (1545).

⁷⁹ Mario Nizzoli or Nizolio (1498-1576); Giraldi refers to his *Observationes in M. T. Ciceronem* (1536), reprinted as *Thesaurus Ciceronianus*.

⁸⁰ Francesco Alunno (*ca*. 1485-1556); Giraldi refers to his *Os-*

servationi sopra il Petrarcha (1539), a gloss on the *Canzoniere;* and *Richezze della lingua volgare sopra il Boccaccio* (1546-1548), a dictionary in ten books. Giraldi also cites the title of a third work, the *Fabrica.*

[81] Giraldi apparently refers to Dante and Petrarch.

[82] This is a reference to an ancient anecdote of Plato and Anniceris, who bought Plato out of slavery and set him free. Anniceris, who was noted for skill in driving a chariot, is said to have driven his chariot into the Academy and to have maneuvered it so well that he went about several turns without allowing the wheels to move out of their original track. This feat reputedly prompted Plato to remark that it was impossible for one who put so much attention on unimportant matters to understand what was really important. Lucian included this story of Anniceris's feat with the four-horse chariot in "Demosthenes, an Encomium." Other details about Anniceris appear in Aelian, *Varia Historia*, B.27; Olympiodorus, *Commentary on the First Alcibiades of Plato*, 2.122-24, and *Commentary on Plato's Gorgias*, XLI.8; Suidas's Lexicon, IV.141 under "Plato." Diogenes Laertius relates the well-known incident of the freeing of Plato from slavery by Anniceris in "Plato," III, 19-20.

For Pages 53 to 70

[83] The sonnet is indeed nonsense as the following "literal" translation will show. "Happier than a tiger my thoughts, discerning my heart, which among learned bosoms entirely holds a thought, since it loads on it the true and the foolish mistake, they flee the evil events. And although it should be blamed by the old demigods wherever all other is a fierce mountain of pride. Alas, already I do not hope to rejoice in that desire that I would like to have. Therefore, wearied by the harsh sound, the soul sprouts ardor in me when it is reaped to the ground and warms up, now here, now there, the hot frost, and I lose trace of a green flower; for me scorn hid it in a little veil taken by mutilated error from the grave corpse; though he who holds the palm of the mortal frauds may yearn with force to lead to the impious end the bitter rind."

[84] "From him who undertakes to interpret the Sibyls came the suspicion and the fear that now afflicts the heart of him who bows down and adores, that he will not be able to have tranquil hours. And so the Cruelty sends him effronteries, thousands upon thousands, that she would have the lover delay who lives in fire, deprived of life. What good to ask him why he does not complain? Ah, divine justice, why cannot you do what the gods do? What fierce spirit was it that brought this plague into the world? Alas, would I were at this moment put in the bottom of Acheron, were united with the myrtle and made a deadly shade with its branches."

[85] Marsilio Ficino's *Il libro dello amore* (1474; first written in Latin, 1469), commentary on Plato's *Symposium*, was summarized

Editorial Notes

in a canzone by Girolamo Benivieni. This canzone was then expounded in a prose commentary by Pico della Mirandola.

[86] Claudio Tolomei (1492-1555 or 1557); his chief work was *Versi e regole della nuova poesia toscana* (1539), to which Giraldi apparently refers.

[87] Hierocles of Alexandria, the Latin title of his work is *Commentarius in Aurea Carmina Pythagoreorum*.

[88] The Greek philosopher. A long catalog of his works is appended to his life in Diogenes Laertius, VII. Except for a few fragments, these are lost. Precisely where Giraldi derived what he says of Chrysippus as an allegorizer of Homer and to which of his works he refers is uncertain. Diogenes records two that seem probable, "Of Poems" and "On the Right Way of Reading Poetry." Plutarch seems to have used the latter in his "How to Study Poetry" (*Moralia*, 14D-F—37A-B). At one point in this work Plutarch censures Chrysippus for wresting words ingeniously (31E); at another point he says that Chrysippus has rightly indicated how a poet's statements can be given wider application (34B). At any rate, from some source Giraldi was aware of Chrysippus's reputation as an allegorizer of Homer.

[89] Cristoforo Landino (1424-1492) was so embued with Neoplatonism that he conceived of poetry as allegorical and involved "arcani e divini sensi," as in his commentary on the *Aeneid* (1478).

[90] *Poetics*, 1456a, 34—1456b, 8.

[91] In his earlier *Discorso intorno al comporre delle comedie et delle tragedie*.

[92] Pietro Bembo, *Prose della volgar lingua* (in three books).

[93] See note 80 above.

[94] Giangiorgio Trissino, *Poetica*, Divisione V.

[95] Probably refers to *Ars Poetica*, 438-52.

[96] *Canzoniere*, No. 151. "No weary pilot ever fled to port from a dark and stormy sea-wave as I flee from the dark and troubled thought where this mighty desire spurs and inclines me."

[97] *Canzoniere*, No. 106, ll. 1 and 6. "A new small angel balanced on her wings" (1. 6); "[She threw] a woven silk [before me] in the grass; whence the way is green."

[98] *Stanze*, No. 26. "How much the heaven ought to show of it in a thousand years."

[99] "Let him [Love] look once into your beautiful eyes and he may then run away fast or slowly, as he can."

[100] "Let him [Love] once stop to marvel at you and then run away, if he can, with freed soul."

[101] *Orlando Furioso*, 24.45. "This author, whose name I do not mention, writes that they had not gone thence a day's journey, when Odorico, to get out of that scrape, against every pledge and

every oath given, threw a noose around Gabrina's neck and left her hanging on an elm; and that a year hence (but he does not name the place) Almonio played the same trick on him."

[102] *Stanze*, No. 16, ll. 1-4. "What trust of having peace without love, without which one never has a happy life; he makes the saints to flee his laws, as a deadly thing is avoided and feared."

[103] *Orlando Furioso*, 1.11. "He had his cuirass on his back, his helmet on his head, his sword on his flank, and his shield on his arm; and he ran through the forest more lightly than the half-naked peasant after the red cloak."

[104] "I therefore give you this counsel with faith."

[105] *Stanze*, No. 49, ll. 1, 5, and 6. "Come then, with white hair and severe brow, troublesome and feeble old age."

[106] "Other [nymphs?] with their Tritons in beautiful dances, bare of arms and breasts, filled with fears and hopes the gods who had entered the dance with them; and as their desire ever mounted, they kindle new flames in burning hearts, nor did it help them to be of cold humors."

[107] *Orlando Furioso*, 12.49, ll. 1-6. "The prince of Anglant was likewise wholly charmed, except in one place; he could be wounded on the soles of his feet, but he guarded them with great care. The rest [of their bodies] was harder than the diamond (if report does not depart from the truth)."

[108] Giraldi's heroic poem *Dell' Hercole*, First Canto, Stanza 83. "So, as soon as you open your eyes (which you cannot delay much longer), you will see clearly that this fellow would have entangled you in insipid delights with his flatteries and that (for what pleasure falls upon you therefrom) you will be buried alive among vanities and dead to this life, which Idonia gives, and inasmuch as he does, is totally displeased."

[109] Marco Antonio Flaminio (1498-1550), imitated Catullus and Horace in his verse; Cicero in his prose; chief poetical works, *Lusus Pastorales* and *Paraphrases in Triginta Psalmos*.

[110] The Phalaecean (Phalaecian), often called Hendecasyllabic, the principal meter of Catullus's poems, also used frequently by other Roman poets such as Martial. The metrical pattern: $||\stackrel{\perp}{\cup}|\stackrel{\perp}{\cup}\cup|\stackrel{\perp}{\cup}|\stackrel{\perp}{\cup}|\stackrel{\perp}{\cup}||$. For the opening trochee an iambus is frequently substituted. A spondee also occurs frequently in the second foot. As Giraldi's discussion indicates, the meter was much cultivated by Renaissance Latin poets.

[111] Giovanni Pontano (1426?-1503); known academically as Jovianus Pontanus.

[112] Michele Marullo (*ca*. 1440-1500); his *Hymni et Epigrammata* was published at Firenze in 1497; he imitated Catullus and Lucretius.

Editorial Notes

¹¹³ One of the lesser figures of the famous family whose name he bears; better known members were Donato and Pietro.

¹¹⁴ *Stanze*, No. 42. "Why does it please to possess cities, kingdoms, and live in palaces with much labor? To have servants about ready for command and chests of much treasure? To be sung to by fine minstrels, to be clothed in purple, to eat on gold? And to equal the sun in beauty, lying meanwhile in a bed—cold and alone?"

¹¹⁵ *Stanze*, No. 24. "This one [Love] breathed desire in your father, with which, as God pleased, to adorn the world and to delight our eyes with the sight of your beauty born on earth; nor can tongues or inks reckon it; nor do so many waters roll in the sea as Love pours from your beautiful eyes high and various joy, peace, sweetness, and grace."

¹¹⁶ Tibullus, III, 7 (or IV, 1)—the *Panegyricus Messalae*.

¹¹⁷ *Stanze*, No. 45. "O how sweet it is, as Love clasps him."

¹¹⁸ "To know, as one color may paint two faces as a bridle governing two wishes."

¹¹⁹ *Stanze*, No. 48. "So you find there seeking another."

¹²⁰ "Then, since you yourself exiled love, are your fires of such good origin?"

¹²¹ *Canzoniere*, No. 309. "Love, after causing my tongue to be free . . ./ Wants me to paint to those who do not see."

¹²² *Canzoniere*, No. 222. "Merry and thoughtful, escorted, alone,/ Ladies who in conversing go about."

¹²³ *Orlando Furioso*, 6.4, l. 4. "He glittered with such goodness and such valor."

¹²⁴ *Orlando Furioso*, 6.31, ll. 3-4. "By that beautiful lady, that one who holds the better part of me, I promise you."

¹²⁵ *Canzoniere*, No. 18. "When I am pulled and drawn toward that side."

¹²⁶ *Stanze*, No. 38. "This one, wandering here and there."

¹²⁷ *Stanze*, No. 26.

¹²⁸ *Orlando Furioso*, 1.54. "Filled with soft and amorous desire, he ran to his lady, to his divinity, who held him close with her arms about his neck—which in Cathay she perhaps would not have done. Having him with her, she turned her thought to her paternal kingdom, to her native retreat. Suddenly revived in her the hope of soon seeing again her sumptuous palace."

¹²⁹ "How could I not know my benign heavenly one?"

¹³⁰ *Canzoniere*, No. 157. "That ever-cruel, ever-honored day."

¹³¹ L. 7. "Made one doubt whether woman or goddess."

¹³² *Orlando Furioso*, 41.19-20. "Ruggiero, seeing the captain and the owner and the others hurriedly abandon the ship, just as he was, in his coat without armor, planned to escape in the skiff; but found it so loaded with people, and so many came then [to join

them], that the waters went beyond the limit; and the boat, too heavily freighted, went to the bottom with all its load.

"To the bottom of the sea, and with it dragged those who, trusting in it, left the larger vessel. Then they were heard calling on Heaven for help with dolorous cries, when the sea, full of wrath and disdain, came and suddenly blocked the whole passage by which the lament and the plaintive shriek came out."

For Pages 96 to 117

133 The three Giraldi refers to are probably Nos. 55, 72, and 126 of the *Canzoniere*.

134 "One for him and he for the other rejoices."—"He shrinks from her and I am in despair."—"Ifi, who loving another, was so abhorred."—"Issifile comes then, and she too grieves."—"When you come to roll your eyes."

135 "Nor work to smoothe with my file."—"I lived; nor did I distress them or others."—"But I shall be beneath in a dry forest."—"When I knew who were more secure."

136 *Canzoniere*, No. 47, l. 7.

137 *Ars Poetica*, 46-71.

138 Giovanni della Casa (1503-1556) wrote sonnets and canzoni. His best known work in its time was his prose treatise *Galateo overo De Costumi*, on behavior in polite society.

139 Bartolomeo Cavalcanti (1503-1562), to whose *La Retorica divisa in sette libri* Giraldi refers. The earliest edition seems to be that of 1559. Giraldi apparently knew the work earlier, perhaps in MS.

140 Benedetto Varchi (1503-1565), best known for his history of Florence in sixteen books covering the period 1527-1538. Varchi also wrote a number of plays, dialogues, translations from the classics, and poems, including pastorals, to which Giraldi refers.

141 *Stanze*, No. 35.

142 *Asolani*, Bk. Two, No. XVI. "Never such a thief of love nor one so swift."

143 *Canzoniere*, No. 29. "Green clothes or bright red or dark or purple."

144 *Asolani*, Bk. Two, No. XXVIII. "To feed the great hungers that, in such a long fast, you give me, O Love."

145 "The thought that burdens me."

146 *Orlando Furioso*, 23.113. "The violent pain remained within."

147 *Orlando Furioso*, 26.93. "The first and last day that he fights."

148 This stanza occurs in Canto 27.101.

149 "Paris trembled and Seine became tumultous at his shrill voice, at this horrible shriek; the sound echoed even to the forest of Ardennes, so that all the wild beasts left their lairs. The Alps heard, and the mount of Cévennes, the shores of Blaye and of Arles and of Rouen; Rhone and Saône heard, Garonne and the Rhine; mothers clutched their children to their bosoms."

Editorial Notes

[150] As in *Institutes of Oratory*, X, 23.
[151] *Canzoniere*, No. 57. "My lucky chances are lazy and slothful to come."
[152] No. 57, l. 4, "And they run like a tiger when they leave."
[153] *Canzoniere*, No. 90. "The golden hair was loosened in the breeze."
[154] *Canzoniere*, No. 33. "The star of love had just begun to shine."
[155] *Canzoniere*, No. 225. "Twelve women gracefully reclined."
[156] *Canzoniere*, No. 268. "What shall I do? What do you counsel, Love."
[157] "My canzone, not [a canzone], but a lamentation, you are not fit to be among merry folk—a widow, without comfort, in black cloak."
[158] *Canzoniere*, No. 1, l. 11. "So that I feel ashamed of my own name."
[159] *Canzoniere*, No. 304. "When my heart [was eaten] by the amorous worms."
[160] *Prose*, Secondo Libro (*Opere in Volgare*, ed. Marti, pp. 337-38).
[161] *Institutes of Oratory*, X, i, 90.
[162] *Thebaid*, XII, 810-11.
[163] Giraldi apparently refers to Ercole Strozza (1473-1508), son of Tito Vespasiano Strozza (1424-1505). The other person known as Strozza the Younger (Giovambattista Strozza) was born in 1551 and died in 1634 and thus could not be referred to in the *Discorso*, dated 1549, published 1554.
[164] In the *De Oratore* the art of the actor Roscius is often discussed in relation to the art of oratory.
[165] Lactantius (Lucius Caelius Lactantius Firmianus), Christian apologist of the 4th century, often called the Christian Cicero. There were several editions of his *De divinis institutionibus libri septem* in the early sixteenth century (1513, 1515, 1524, 1532, 1535, 1548).
[166] *Asolani*, I, xxiv.
[167] *Canzoniere*, No. 332.
[168] Jacopo Sadoleto (1477-1547); among his works is a hexameter poem on the discovery of the Laocoon, which Giraldi refers to.
[169] *Rhetoric*, III, ii, 6; III, iii, 2; *Poetics*, 1457b, 2; 1458a, 22; 1459a, 11.
[170] *Canzoniere*, No. 189. "My ship is sailing, full of oblivion."
[171] *Canzoniere*, No. 40. "If Love or Death does not give some harm."
[172] *Canzoniere*, No. 217. "I once desired with such a just complaint."

¹⁷³ To whom Giraldi addressed the *Discorso . . . delle comedie et delle tragedie.*
¹⁷⁴ *Canzoniere,* No. 189, l. 9. "A rain of tears, a fog of scorns."
¹⁷⁵ *Canzoniere,* No. 217.
¹⁷⁶ Line 16 (first line of the 6th terza rima). "My four steeds I groom faithfully."
¹⁷⁷ *Stanze,* No. 5, l. 6. "So much did we respect and honor one another."
¹⁷⁸ L. Cornelius Sisenna (cf. *Brutus,* lxxiv, 259-60).
¹⁷⁹ Cf. *Partitiones Oratoriae,* ii, 7 and 12.
¹⁸⁰ In *Rhetoric,* III, iii, 2, three phrases of Alcidamas are quoted as examples of frigidity.
¹⁸¹ Andrea Navagero (Naugerius)—1483-1529—to whose Latin poems *Lusus* ("Playful Pieces"), Giraldi probably refers.
¹⁸² Francesco Maria Molza (1489-1544); Giraldi doubtless refers to his *Ad Sodales.*
¹⁸³ *Rhetoric,* III, iii, 7.
¹⁸⁴ *Rime,* No. 35.
¹⁸⁵ "Death seemed fair in her fair face."
¹⁸⁶ *Canzoniere,* No. 225.
¹⁸⁷ *Triumph of Love,* IV, 152-54. "Never boiled Vulcan [volcano], Lipari or Ischia or Stromboli or Mongibel with such fury; miserable indeed is he who risks such a game."
¹⁸⁸ "Gentle Eurus, who tosses the golden curled tangles, now here, now there, about her beautiful face."
¹⁸⁹ "Triumphal, glorious, and fortunate bark, you that bear the beautiful Siren across the sea, how many have been taken by you? And how many have died? I see you go laden with trophies of love. Wiser is the way of Ulysses, who passes by you, deaf to the sound, blind to the beautiful and cunning attendants. Alas, why did I not yearn before for the short days when without you the Fate was weary with spinning? Marveling I see the fishes gather and the birds fly all about, the winds and the waters come to a smooth harmony before your beautiful face. The Siren of the sky was suddenly silent; the pole paused and the day was doubled; so pleasing was it to everyone to hear and see her."
¹⁹⁰ *Canzoniere,* No. 304, ll. 13-14. "With words I would have broken a stone and made it weep with tenderness."
¹⁹¹ "That make mountains shake and rivers stop flowing."
¹⁹² Cf. *Epistles,* II, i, 170 ff.; *Ars Poetica,* 270 ff.
¹⁹³ His *Discorso . . . delle comedie et delle tragedie.*
¹⁹⁴ *Peri Ideon,* B.3 ("Peri Apheleias"—"Of Simplicity"); ed. Teubner, 1913, pp. 322-29.
¹⁹⁵ *Moralia,* 34C ("How to Study Poetry").
¹⁹⁶ "He who does another a favor ought to be sure to lease it to

him, for the ingrate often tries with heavy anguish to reward him well; and everyone indebted to a kind man, on his worse side, endeavors to detract from him; the wicked one is not changed by a benefit, nor does the ungrateful man care for a kind service."

[197] This familiar Renaissance doctrine was based on a wrenched reading of Horace's phrase *Ut pictura poesis* (Ars Poetica, 361).

[198] *Works and Days*, 349-50; Cicero cites this passage in *De Officiis*, I, 15.

[199] Giraldi translates here a speech of Damoetas, one of the persons in *Eclogue* III (cf. *Eclogues*, III, 23-24). Probably Giraldi derived this from one of the allegorical interpretations of the *Eclogues*.

INDEX

Acciaivoli, Giacopo: diction and meter, 96
Alunno, Francesco, 64, 76
Anniceris of Cyrene. See Plato
Apostrophe (mark of elision), 174
Ariosto, Lodovico. See *Orlando Furioso*
Aristotle. See *Ethics, Poetics*
Art: concealing art, 122-25
Aspirate *h*: use of, 171-72
Atheneus: Tantalus myth, 47
Ausonius, 165

Bembo, Pietro: sweetness and gravity, 118-19; mentioned, xiv, 4, 166
—*Asolani*: rhymes, 107-108, 115-16
—*Prose*: rivals Aristotle's *Rhetoric*, xix; placement of words, 94-95
—*Stanze*: quoted, 89, 96-97, 98-99, 100; avoided repetition of rhymes, 102-103
Bibbiena (Bernardo Dovisi): use of witticism in *Calandria*, 149
Boccaccio, Giovanni: epithets, 144
Boiardo, Matteo Maria: followed nature, 122, 174-75; mentioned, xix, 9, 10, 122

Canto: origin of, 7-8; linking of, 35-37
Castiglione, Baldassare: Strozza's poem attributed to, 147
Catullus: use of hendecasyllabic Phalacean, 95; varied caesurae, 98
—*Epithalamium of Peleus and Thetis*, 45-46
Cavalcanti, Bartolomeo: *Rhetoric*, 113
Chrysippus, 184n

Cicero: *Brutus*, 7; *Tusculan Disputations*, 7; use of foreign words, 154; mentioned, 15
Cino da Pistoia, 124
Citolini, Alessandro, 4
Claudian: *Panegyrics*, 24; imitated by Politian, 53
Coluthus the Theban: *The Rape of Helen*, 46

Dante: criticism of his time, 53; *Banquet*, 70; compared with Petrarch, 113-14; sweetness in, 124; plebeian words in, 136-37
Dares Phrygius, 21
Da Vinci, Leonardo, 160-63
Decorum: theory of, xvi-xvii, 56-62; in Homer, 28-32, 58-59, 166; in Vergil, 29-32; in Lucan's *Pharsalia*, 60; in modern heroic poem, 60-62; in Trissino's *Italia*, 60; in Vida's *Christiad*, 61
Della Casa, Giovanni: good diction in, 113; mentioned, xix
Dictys Cretensis. See Dares Phrygius
Digressions, 53-54
Diodorus Siculus, 51-52
Divus (diva): use of, 170

Elocution, 72-73
Enargeia: defined, 55; misconceived by Trissino, 135
Enthusiasm *(furor poeticus)*, 27, 166
Estienne, Robert: *Thesaurus*, 64
Ethics, 165

Fable: in Romances, 9; importance of, 10-11; concerned with perfection, 167
Ficino, Marsilio: and Platonism, 70
Fictionality: essential in poetry, xv

191

Figures of speech: similitudes, 135; comparisons, 135, 141-43; adjuncts (epithets), 135, 143-46, 175-76; hyperbole, 135, 146-48, 177; metaphor, 136-39, 175-76; consistency in, 137; absurd, 138; difference between metaphor and similitude, 139; difference between adjunct and metaphor, 143; bad use of, 144-45; oxymora, 145, 177
Flaccus, Valerius: unnatural, 121
Flaminio, Marco Antonio, 95

Giraldi, Giovambattista: *The Journey of Juno to Neptune*, quoted, 91-92; *Dell' Hercole*, quoted, 92

Hermogenes: on sentences, 150
Heroic poem: modern, xix, xx, 39-40; definition of, 10-11; subject matter of, 13, 44-47; beginning point of, 19; unity in, 21-23, 37-39
Homer: decorum in, xiv; *Margites*, 10; not a good example, 31-32; allegorizing of, 33-34; commentary on, 71
Horace: *utile et dulci*, xviii; begin *in medias res*, 17, 18; single action, 20; hyperbole in *Odes*, 177; mentioned, 51, 62, 74

Imitation (mimesis): in poetic theory, xvii-xviii, 26-27, 48; of excellencies, 27-28; as emulation, 126-28; of words, 127-28
Invention: importance in Giraldi, xv
Invocation: in heroic poem, 42-44

Jonson, Ben: "needful rules," xiv; *Bartholomew Fair*, xxii
Judgment: ways of learning, 25-28

Landino, Cristoforo, 71
Lucretius: tempered nature with art, 121-22
Lully, Raymond, 63

Macrobius, 34, 71
Maggio, Vincentio, 5

Marullo, Michele: use of stanza and hendecasyllabics, 95
Maximus Tyrius, 148
Mazzoni, Jacopo: *Discorso in defesa della Commedia del divino poeta Dante*, xix
Milton, John: *Paradise Lost*, xv
Mimesis. *See* Imitation
Minturno, Antonio: *L'Arte Poetica*, xix
Molza, Francesco Maria, 145

Nature: and art, 120-26
Navagero, Andrea, 145
Nizzolio, Mario: guide for writers, 64

Oratory: theory of, xv
Organic: theory of, xv-xvi; poem like living body, 15-16; relation of parts, 24-25; "soul" of a work, 134-35
Orlando Furioso: defense of, xiii, 1; and *romanzi*, xiv; faults in, 24; indecorums in, 31; quoted, 90, 91, 92, 101; rhymes in, 103, 104-105, 116-17, 172-73; diction in, 116-17; revisions of, 170-74; mentioned, xix, xxi, 9
Ovid: followed nature more than art, 121; mentioned, xix, 165
—*Metamorphoses*: multiple unity in, 20, 40-41; feigning in, 45, 46-47; compared with Romances, 53

Patronyms: in heroic poem, 41-42
Petrarch: allegoresis of poems, 67-68; compared with Dante, 113-14; art of, 122
—*Canzoniere*: sonnets on Rome, 53; canzone on Italy, 53; quoted, 88, 99, 165; diction in, 114, 118, 119, 136; use of adverbs in, 146; good usage in, 173; imagery in, 176, 177
—*Triumphs*: use of rhymes, 107; diction in, 113-14
—*De remediis utriusque fortunae*: overuse of sentences in, 152
Philostratus, 47
Pico della Mirandola, 70

Pisander, 20
Plato, 15, 67, 168, 183n
Plautus: use of witticisms in, 149
Pliny the Elder, 35
Plutarch: on Homer, 14; on Enargeia, 135; *Moralia*, 152
Poet: compared with philosopher, 34, 168; and the rules, 48; a maker or feigner, 50, 51; and virtue, 52-53; requisites of, 157-58; criticism of 158-59, 163-64, 177; and knowledge, 160-61
Poetics, 5, 12, 14, 20, 50, 51, 52, 62, 74, 165
Poetry: nature and art requisite for, 93-94; and philosophy, 124-26; measure and decorum in, 152-53; and painting, 153
Politian, xix, 53
Pontano: excellence in feigning, 50; use of hendecasyllabics, 95; imitation of Flaccus, 121
Pulci, Luigi: *Morgante*, 10; repetition in, 102

Quintilian, 35, 121
Quintus of Calabria, 45

Repetition: avoidance of, 101; laudable, 101-102; in *Orlando Furioso*, 106-107
Rhetorical schemes and tropes; absurdity and futility of, 62-67
Rhymes: and heroic poem, 80-82; and meaning, 81, 86-88; used artistically, 88-92; in *Orlando Furioso*, 103-105; repetition of, 107-108
Riccio, Bartholomeo, 64
Ruggieri, Boniface, 1-2

Sadoletto, Jacopo: *Laocoon*, 133
Sannazaro, Jacopo: imitation of Flaccus, 121; *Arcadia*, 144
Seneca, Lucius Annaeus: *Moralia*, 152
Sentences (sententiae): in tragedies, 149; in comedies, 149; types of, 150-51; Plutarch's definition of, 151; as extended statements, 151-52; overuse of, 152

Servius, 35, 167
Shakespeare, William: *King Lear*, xxii
Sidney, Philip, xvii
Spenser, Edmund: *The Faerie Queene*, xv, xxii
Stanza: terza rima, 82-83; ottava rima, 82-83, 85, 95-101; linking of, 100-101
Statius, 121
Strozza, Ercole: quoted, 147; mentioned, 188n
Suidas: on epic and history, 19

Tasso, Torquato: *Discorsi del poema eroico*, xxi; *Gerusalemme Liberata*, xv
Tense, shifting of: in *Orlando Furioso*, 105-107; in Dante and Petrarch, 106
Theocritus, 113
Tibullus: use of hexameters, 98; excessive epithets, 144-45; mentioned, xix
Tolomei, Claudio, 70
Tragedy: and modern subjects, 12; and heroic poem, 72
Trissino, Giangiorgio: *Italia liberata dai Goti*, 30-31; digression in, 48; mentioned, xix
Tucca (and Varius): omitted lines from *Aeneid* as indecorous, 33

Valerius Maximus, 7
Varchi, Benedetto: and diction, 113
Vergil: *Georgics*, 13; *Eclogues*, 35, 164; Landino on, 71; mentioned, xiv, 8, 113, 166
—*Aeneid*: imitation of Homer, 17-18, 142-43, 176; decorum in, 34-35; feigning in, 45, 167; mentioned, 51, 168
Verisimilitude: the traditional as, 49
Verse: hendecasyllabic, 77; *sdruccioli*, 77-78, 80; unrhymed *(sciolti)*, 78-82; hendecasyllabic Phalaecean, 95; elision in, 109-11
Vida, Marco Girolamo; *Ars Poetica*, 50; *Christiad*, 182n

Words: importance in choice of, 74-75; license in use of, 111-12, 113, 174; new, 111-16, 140-41; effects of, 117-20; choice of, 119-20; foreign, 135, 154, 177; popu-

Words (*continued*):
lar, 136; transferred or metaphorical, 136

Xenophon: *Cyropedia*, 18

www.ingramcontent.com/pod-product-compliance
Lightning Source LLC
Chambersburg PA
CBHW022100160426
43198CB00008B/292